Continuing Education
for Adults
through
the American Public Library

1833–1964

Continuing Education
for Adults
through
the American Public Library

1833-1964

ROBERT ELLIS LEE

**AMERICAN
LIBRARY ASSOCIATION**

Chicago, 1966

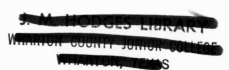

Preface

The establishment of the American public library during the middle of the last century was considered to be a civic and social innovation, providing, as it did, a publicly supported institution based on the belief that men could use recorded knowledge and ideas for the advancement of themselves and the improvement of society. The objective of this new institution was primarily educational and was implemented by making books accessible to adults of all classes. The educational role of the public library was to serve as a means by which persons in all walks of life could continue their education through reading if they were so inclined. Self-development was the all-pervading concept upon which the library was founded, and adult education the primary objective, even though the term "adult education" was not used.

As public libraries increased in number and in the size of their collections, services other than those stemming from the educational objective began to develop. Recreational reading was introduced as a service in a number of libraries during the 1870's, and the provision of this type of material gradually became accepted by most librarians and patrons as a regular library function. Informational reference service by public libraries began during the 1880's; it consisted of answering questions, locating facts, and directing patrons to books that could be used in pursuing inquiries. This service, provided at first on a limited basis, eventually became an established, integral function of the public library.

Although each public library in the United States has always been free to determine its own objectives and to pursue them in its own way, the objectives held in common by the majority of public libraries are educa-

v

tion, information, and recreation. These three objectives are interrelated, and no one of them can be considered in isolation. For this reason, a discussion of the evolution of any one of the objectives of the American public library system must take into account its relation to the other two.

A multiplicity of factors, operating over a long period of time, contributed to the evolving concept of the educational commitment and the pattern of the educational services of the public library. This evolutionary process has never been recorded and analyzed. The lack of historical perspective concerning the educational work of public libraries has been costly in terms of time, money, and labor. Even a preliminary examination of library literature reveals the duplication of effort stemming from insufficient knowledge of previous work. Without an adequate basis of historical fact, it is difficult to obtain a clear perspective of the form, substance, and direction of what is called "library adult education."

The purpose of this study, originally prepared in partial fulfillment of the requirements for the degree of Doctor of Philosophy at the University of Chicago, 1963, has been to describe the evolution of the adult educational commitment of the American public library, with particular attention to the most prevalent interpretation of the library's educational objective and the most common educational services provided in each period discussed. The more specific intent has been to determine in what way the interpretation and implementation of the library's adult educational commitment changed between 1833 and 1964. The investigation was based on the assumption that a clear perspective of the library's adult educational work could not be obtained by studying this aspect of library operations as a separate and isolated entity. Therefore, the evolution of the library's adult educational commitment has been traced against the background of the institutional development of the American public library, *i.e.,* in relation to the adoption of general library practices and policies, the emergence of other library objectives, and the developmental pattern of library services.

The present volume is not a definitive history of library adult education; it does not describe all the notable adult educational services and programs of individual libraries. Rather, it attempts to identify the major stages in the growth of the adult educational work of public libraries, to describe the main lines of this development in relation to the institutional history of public libraries, and to analyze the dominant features of the evolving philosophy of library adult education. It is the author's hope that this initial study may be useful for subsequent and more detailed investigations of this subject by others.

This work could not have been completed without the help and cooperation of a number of persons. To these persons I am deeply indebted, and also to many others who contributed by offering suggestions and providing materials.

I especially wish to express my gratitude to the members of my doctoral committee at the University of Chicago: Professor Cyril O. Houle, Professor Herman G. Richey, and Lester Asheim, formerly Dean of the Graduate Library School and now Director of the American Library Association Office of International Relations. I am also indebted to many of my colleagues in the library profession for their help and suggestions.

My wife Helen and son Stephen deserve special words of appreciation for their moral support and helpful comments during the years this study was in preparation.

Robert Ellis Lee
Chairman, Department of Librarianship
Kansas State Teachers College
Emporia, Kansas

Contents

Chapter		Page
I	Collecting and Preserving Books, 1833–1875	1
II	Organizing Resources, 1876–1897	14
III	Extending Services, 1898–1919	31
IV	Serving the Individual, 1920–1940	45
V	Strengthening Democracy, 1941–1956	72
VI	Moving Forward, 1957–1964	89
VII	Summary and Conclusions	112
Notes		129
A Selective Bibliography		147
Index		155

Collecting
and Preserving Books
1833–1875

The public library was the first tax-supported agency established in the United States for the informal education of adults. It was organized specifically to provide a means by which mature individuals could continue to learn through their own efforts. The educational commitment of the public library of today is intimately linked by tradition with the ideals upon which the American public library was founded. Thus, a preliminary view of the origin of the public library and of the beliefs upon which it was established, and an appreciation of the stages through which it has progressed, are needed for a clear understanding of the nature of the educational aims and the form of the educational services of the modern public library.

Beginnings of the American Public Library

The origin and early development of the American public library cannot be attributed to any single influence. A number of forces—social, political, and cultural—contributed to its emergence and subsequently determined the nature of its educational commitment. The most important ones may be singled out for mention.

Need for Public Libraries

The first half of the nineteenth century was the period when the new American nation both established itself and demonstrated its fundamental unity. It was a time of many social movements, of upheaval, and of a continuing effort to establish the distinctive cultural pattern of the United States. During the early part of the century a belief was widely held among influential citizens that all men were endowed with unlimited rational capacity and that every human being possessed both a natural right to knowledge and the potentiality for achieving it.[1] These persons thought that even the ordinary man, through education and reading,[2] could acquire scientific and other knowledge; that if suitable means could be found for individuals to develop their inherent abilities, the continuing improvement of society would be assured.

With the granting of male suffrage, the American people began to express themselves in political activity. The growth of democratic participation was perhaps inevitable, but it was incompatible with one of the assumptions of democratic government—*informed* citizens are essential to the vitality of democracy. It was recognized that the unenlightened persons to whom the privilege of citizenship had been extended could not be expected to uphold democratic institutions unless they understood them. These persons, as well as the new immigrants who had to be assimilated into the political and cultural patterns of America, should be able to understand and appreciate the founding fathers' struggle for freedom, comprehend the problems of government, think independently, and vote intelligently. Thus, a need was evident for a continuing source of information, free from censorship, which would provide the citizenry with the means necessary for a sound, collective judgment on public affairs.

The steady development of public school education in America helped to produce an increased number of literate young people. The school fostered in some young adults an interest in various fields of knowledge and provided them with a method for the continuing study of subjects. The seeds of inquiry had been sown. But when these young people left school, those who could not buy their own books were barred from further learning. Clearly the efforts of the public schools would be wasted if no means were available for the working adult to continue his education. An agency was needed that would provide, on a free and equal basis, the means of self-education.

During the 1820's and 1830's, experiments in education for adults— such as the American Lyceum movement, which provided inspirational lectures, concerts, and entertainments, and the widespread literary and debating societies—stimulated an interest in cultural development. In the pursuit of these and other interests books were indispensable. These new educational activities created a need for providing mature men and women with the means for reading and studying the cultural and literary heritage of their country.

In the same period, industrialization and increasing urbanization gave rise to new social and moral problems: crime, alcoholism, gambling, prostitution, and child delinquency. The leading citizens, convinced that a republic could not survive unless its people were virtuous as well as intelligent, were seeking ways of suppressing vice and implanting good morals. They asserted that, in addition to the moral instruction provided by the public school, a public library would be a potent enemy of crime and a continuing means of moral elevation for the working adult. It would be an attractive, cultural establishment that would help to create an interest in lofty, noble, and religious endeavors. It would provide a rational form of activity. Moreover, a public library, it was argued, would be less expensive to establish and maintain than a prison or reformatory.

Although societal forces created the need for an agency such as the public library, certain conditions had to be present in a community before a public library could be established. These conditions, in the order of their importance, were: financial ability to set up and maintain a public library; energetic and progressive leaders who recognized the need for such an agency and were able to persuade the majority of their fellow citizens to impose an additional tax on themselves to support it; a public school system; and a sufficient number of educated adults who had a need for reading.

Early Development

On April 9, 1833, the citizens of Peterborough, New Hampshire, without the sanction of state legislation, voted to set aside for the purchase of library books a portion of the state bank tax, which was distributed among New Hampshire towns for schools or "other purposes of education." Thus, the first American town library, open to the public and continuously supported by tax funds, was begun.[3] This new civic institution, however, did not suddenly appear on the American scene. It was the product of almost a century and a half of experimentation in the development of three major types of semipublic libraries: parish and parochial libraries, social libraries (proprietary, subscription, mechanics' and mercantile libraries), and circulating libraries.[4]

The establishment of the Peterborough Library in 1833 was significant in that it set a precedent in the use of public funds. Other free libraries were established during the next two decades in some of the small towns in Massachusetts, New Hampshire, and New York State.[5] The organization of free libraries was relatively slow, however, until 1854 when the city of Boston—one of the large and culturally important cities of the country—established a public library. This marked the turning point in the history of the public library movement in the United States. The organization of a public library by a major metropolitan community, and the formulation by its founders of a rationale for free public library service, provided the impetus needed to set the public library concept into motion.

Founding of the
Boston Public Library

In 1839, M. Nicholas Marie Alexandre Vattemare, a former actor and ventriloquist who was serving as an emissary of the French government, toured this country with the object of establishing a system for the international exchange of books. After presenting his proposal to President Van Buren and to members of the Congress, he was asked to visit Boston on the assurance of John Quincy Adams "that of all the cities of the New World none are better qualified to appreciate and support the system."[6]

In April, 1841, Vattemare went to Boston and there introduced his program for the exchange of books and a corollary of his plan, which involved the establishment of a free public library. His purpose, according to Josiah Quincy, President of Harvard College and a former mayor of Boston, was "to give the intellectual treasures of the civilized world the same dissemination and equalization which commerce [had] already given to its material ones."[7] Although an enthusiastic response greeted Vattemare's presentation at two public meetings held in Boston in 1841,[8] no official action was then taken. His efforts had no tangible effect in Boston until six years later.

In October, 1847, Mayor Josiah Quincy, Jr., received on behalf of the City a gift of fifty books from the City of Paris. That same month the city council of Boston appointed a joint committee to prepare an acknowledgment to be sent to Paris and to consider the formation of a public library. The members of this committee prepared a report, submitted on October 18, in which they presented the reasons for the establishment of a free library in Boston. "It will tend," they said,

> to interest the people at large in literature and science. It will provide for
> those who are desirous of reading a better class of books than the
> ephemeral literature of the day. It may be the means for developing minds
> that will make their possessors an honor and blessing to their race.
> It will give to the young when leaving school an opportunity to make
> further advances in learning and knowledge. It will, by supplying an
> innocent and praiseworthy occupation, prevent a resort to those scenes
> of amusement that are prejudicial to the elevation of the mind. It will in
> addition to lectures established by Mr. Lowell and the libraries and
> advantages of the neighboring University, tend to make this City the resort
> of learned and scientific men from all sections of the Country,
> increasing the intelligence, the character, and the wealth of the City.
> . . . .
> Linked together as we are by political and business relations the character
> and intelligence of the people in every city between Massachusetts
> and Oregon is of vast importance to the citizens of Boston. If a
> free public library is established here our example will be imitated.[9]

Library Legislation

In January, 1848, the city council directed Mayor Quincy to apply to the legislature for power to enable the city to establish and maintain a public library. On May 18, 1848, the Massachusetts Legislature passed an act that enabled the city of Boston "to establish and maintain a Public Library, for the use of its inhabitants."[10] This was the first statute passed by a state governing body authorizing the establishment of a public library as a municipal institution supported by taxation. The following year, the New Hampshire Legislature passed the first general library law permitting "any town in the State to raise and appropriate money for the establishment and maintenance of a public library, and to be open for the free use of every inhabitant of the town, for the general diffusion of intelligence among all classes of the community."[11] On May 24, 1851, a similar act was passed by the Massachusetts Legislature. "The object aimed at in procuring the passage of this Act," wrote the Reverend John B. Wight, a member of the Massachusetts Legislature,

> . . . was not merely to prevent the necessity of special legislation, whenever any city or town might wish to have such a library, but to bring the formation of Free Public Libraries before the public mind, that it might recommend itself to universal adoption as an important supplement to the common schools, academies, and colleges, in the subsequent and life-long education of the whole people.[12]

Securing permissive legislation enabling communities to tax themselves was a necessary first step; the more difficult task, however, was for local authorities and enlightened citizens to implement this legislation by actually establishing libraries and obtaining funds for their maintenance.

Everett and Ticknor

In 1850, Edward Everett, a former President of Harvard College and Senator from Massachusetts, became interested in the plan for a public library, and offered to present his collection of American state papers, public documents, and other works if the city would provide a suitable place for them.[13] In a letter to Mayor Bigelow of Boston, dated June 7, 1851, Everett wrote:

> The first principles of popular government require that the means of education should, as far as possible, be equally within the reach of the whole population. . . . This however is the case only up to the age when School education is at an end. We provide our children with the elements of learning and science, and put it in their power by independent study and research to make further acquisitions of useful knowledge from books—but where are they to find the books in which it is contained? Here the noble principle of equality sadly fails. The sons of the wealthy alone have access to well-stored libraries; while those whose means do not allow them to purchase books are too often debarred

from them at the moment when they would be most useful. We give them
an elementary education, impart to them a taste and inspire them with
an earnest desire for further attainment—which unite in making
books a necessity for intellectual life—and then make no provision
for supplying them.

. . . .

For these reasons I cannot but think that a Public Library, well supplied
with books in various departments of art and science, and open at all
times for consultation and study to the citizens at large, is absolutely
needed to make our admirable system of Public Education complete; and
to continue in some degree through life that happy equality of intellectual
privileges, which now exists in our schools, but terminates with them.[14]

Everett continued by describing the conditions necessary for extending
educational opportunities: if the public schools taught students how to
read and developed in them a continuing curiosity about the world,
public libraries would provide the means for continuing the educational
process throughout life. Everett's assumption was that with the establishment of a public library the knowledge of this world would be at the
disposal of those who could read and who had the incentive to do so.

Everett, in his attempt to establish a free library, was joined by
George Ticknor, a professor of foreign languages at Harvard. In a letter
to Everett, dated July 14, 1851, Ticknor suggested that a public library
"would be the crowning glory of our public schools."[15] He agreed with
Everett on all points concerning a free library except one: the nature of
the book collection. Ticknor maintained that a library should be organized to serve all classes of people and, to achieve this end, popular
books should be provided.[16] He said that the proposed public library

. . . should be adapted to our peculiar character; that is, that it should
come in at the end of our system of free instruction, and be fitted to
continue and increase the effects of that system by the self-culture that
results from reading.

. . . .

Now what seems to me to be wanted in Boston is an apparatus that shall
carry this taste for reading as deep as possible into society, assuming, what I
believe to be true, that it can be carried deeper in our society than in any
other in the world, because we are better fitted for it. To do this I would
establish a library which, in its main department and purpose, should
differ from all free libraries yet attempted; I mean one in which any popular
book . . . should be furnished in such numbers of copies that many
persons, if they desired it, could be reading the same work at the same
time; . . . This appetite for general reading, once formed, will take care of
itself. It will, in the majority of cases, demand better and better books;
and can, I believe, by a little judicious help, rather than by any direct
control or restraint, be carried much higher than is generally thought
possible.[17]

The crucial moment in the establishment of a public library in Boston came in the early part of 1852. On May 24, Everett, Ticknor, and three other citizens were appointed as members of the first board of trustees. Ticknor at first declined to accept the office "unless the library were to be dedicated, in the first instance, rather to satisfying the wants of the less favored classes of the community, than—like all existing libraries— to satisfying the wants of scholars, men of science, and cultivated men generally."[18] No agreement to these terms was made, but Ticknor never- theless accepted the office. The newly formed board of trustees held its first meeting May 31 and appointed a committee consisting of Edward Everett, George Ticknor, Sampson Reed, and Nathaniel Shurtleff "to take into consideration the objects to be obtained by the establishment of a public library, and the best mode of effecting them, and to report thereon."[19] This report, largely written by Ticknor,[20] was submitted and unanimously adopted on July 6, 1852. It laid down the fundamental concept on which the American public library system has since de- veloped and was, according to Jesse H. Shera, the leading authority on this period of public library development,

> . . . the first real credo of the public library. Modified by experience only
> in minor detail, it still stands as the best single statement of the relation of
> the library to the social order. What was said then has been repeated
> many times since, but seldom with equal clarity and precision.[21]

The 1852 report, because of the extensive influence it has had on public library development and because of its explicit definition of the educa- tional function of a public library, will be quoted at length.

The 1852 Report

The purpose of the Boston Public Library, according to the report, was to supplement the city's system of education. Boston provided "a first rate school education, at the public expense, to the entire rising generation."[22] However, and this particular point was emphasized,

> . . . when this object is attained, and it is certainly one of the highest
> importance, our system of public instruction stops. Although the school
> and even the college and the university are, as all thoughtful persons are
> well aware, but the first stages in education, the public makes no provision
> for carrying on the great work. It imparts, with a noble equality of
> privilege, a knowledge of the elements of learning to all its children, but
> it affords them no aid in going beyond the elements. It awakens a taste for
> reading, but it furnishes to the public nothing to be read. It conducts
> our young men and women to that point, where they are qualified
> to acquire from books the various knowledge in the arts and sciences
> which books contain; but it does nothing to put those books within
> their reach. As matters now stand, and speaking with general reference
> to the mass of the community, the public makes no provision whatever, by

which the hundreds of young persons annually educated, as far as
the elements of learning are concerned, at the public expense, can carry
on their education and bring it to practical results by private study.
· ·
The trustees submit, that all the reasons which exist for furnishing
the means of elementary education, at the public expense, apply in an
equal degree to a reasonable provision to aid and encourage the
acquisition of the knowledge required to complete a preparation for
active life or to perform its duties.

· ·
... a free public library is not only seen to be demanded by the wants
of the city at this time, but also seen to be the next natural step to be taken
for the intellectual advancement of this whole community and for
which this whole community is peculiarly fitted and prepared.[23]

The trustees were of the opinion that a public library, like a public
school, would strengthen the "republic government." They reasoned
that (1) the building and maintenance of a free nation rested on the
wisdom of the people who controlled it; (2) the nation placed upon
its electorate an increasing responsibility but had no comprehensive
policy for educating the people beyond common school requirements;
and (3) a nation which granted freedom of choice to its people must,
therefore, provide a means of continuing education which would
ensure that choices would be intelligent.

For it has been rightly judged that,—under political, social and religious
institutions like ours,—it is of paramount importance that the means
of general information should be so diffused that the largest possible
number of persons should be induced to read and understand questions
going down to the very foundations of [the] social order, which are
constantly presenting themselves, and which we, as a people, are constantly
required to decide, and do decide, either ignorantly or wisely. That this
can be done,—that is, that such libraries *can* be collected, and that
they will be used to a much wider extent than libraries have ever been used
before, and with much more important results, there can be no doubt;
and if it can be done *anywhere,* it can be done *here* in Boston; for no
population of one hundred and fifty thousand souls, lying so compactly
together as to be able, with tolerable convenience, to resort to one
library, was ever before so well fitted to become a reading, self-cultivating
population, as the population of our own city is at this moment.[24]

The proposed library, as stated in the report, was conceived of as
an institution

... to which the young people of both sexes, when they leave the
schools, can resort for those works which are needful for research into
any branch of useful knowledge.[25]

The immediate purpose of a public library was to raise the reading
tastes of the majority of citizens through the provision of what Ticknor

called "popular books." The long-range purpose, once general reading standards were raised, was to make the institution

> . . . a great and rich library for men of science, statesmen and scholars, as well as for the great body of the people, many of whom are always successfully struggling up to honorable distinctions and all of whom should be encouraged and helped to do it.[26]

In attempting to achieve these purposes, the trustees

> . . . would endeavor to make the Public Library of the City, as far as possible, the crowning glory of our system of City Schools; or in other words, they would make it an institution, fitted to continue and increase the best effects of that system, by opening to all the means of self culture through books for which these schools have been specially qualifying them.[27]

The report was submitted to the city council during the latter part of July, 1852. Benjamin Seaver, the mayor of Boston, sent a copy of the trustees' report to Joshua Bates, a successful London banker and former resident of Boston. In a letter to Mayor Seaver, dated October 1, 1852, Bates offered $50,000 for the purchase of books if the city would provide a building for the library.[28] Suitable facilities were provided, and the Boston Public Library was officially opened May 2, 1854, to all inhabitants of the city over the age of sixteen.[29]

Educational Rationale

The Boston Public Library came into existence, not because the people demanded a library, but because a small number of learned and influential citizens expressed the need for providing equal educational opportunities for adults. The chief motivating forces were: first, effective leadership and benevolent philanthropy, and, second, a firm belief in the social value of education, with, however, an awareness of the limits of formal education as a permanent means of individual betterment, moral improvement, and political progress.[30] The existing social, economic, and cultural conditions that enabled the founders of the Boston Public Library to put their ideas into practice were: a growing urban area which was rapidly becoming an industrial center; a cultural heritage expressed in a body of literature important enough to be disseminated; and a system of public education producing an increased number of literate adults.

Public education was considered to be the best means of solving social and political problems and the most certain guaranty of continuing progress. The communication of knowledge, it was hoped, would bring about a number of desirable results: improve the personal and vocational competence of individuals; protect and perpetuate republican institutions; dissolve social differences; check demagogues through intelligent use of the ballot; make citizens virtuous as well as intelligent;

maintain the prosperity and well-being of the country; make men more efficient as producers; inculcate respect for property rights; curb radical tendencies; and prevent labor uprisings.[31] These convictions about the ends of education were based on the belief that the well-being of the individual was intimately related to the conditions of society as a whole. The goal was a better society, the barrier was ignorance, and the means—public education.

Most of the ideals, many of the conditions, and some of the assumptions that led to the establishment of the public schools led logically to the establishment of the Boston Public Library. This library was organized for the purpose of providing a means by which the citizens of the community could continue to learn through their own efforts. Its role was to serve as a supplement to the public school system. Its function was to provide adults[32] with equal access to books. And, although never publicly stated, this library was initiated as a municipal experiment. The founders made an assumption about the educational value of books and formulated what was, in fact, a statement of belief concerning what a public library could accomplish. Only the events of the future would indicate whether the ideals of the founders of the Boston Public Library could be achieved.

Growth of Public Libraries

In the period immediately following the establishment of the Boston Public Library, the ideas of Ticknor and Everett were reiterated in many New England communities as the primary reasons for the establishment of a public library.[33] In the 1850's, thirty-five public libraries were organized: thirty in Massachusetts, four in New Hampshire, and one in Maine. During the next decade relatively little progress was made; the Civil War halted the formation of new libraries and the growth of the old. But library development was revitalized between 1870 and 1875, when more public libraries were established than had been in the previous twenty years.

Between 1850 and 1875, the public library movement in the United States began to assume a definite form in the northeastern and midwestern states. Enabling laws for public libraries were enacted in ten states, and free municipal libraries established in eight cities:

Enabling Laws for Public Libraries[34]		Free Municipal Libraries[35]	
Massachusetts	1851	Boston	1854
Maine	1854	Cincinnati	1856
Vermont	1865	Detroit	1865
Ohio	1868	St. Louis	1865
Wisconsin	1868	Cleveland	1868
Connecticut	1869	Louisville	1871
Iowa	1870	Indianapolis	1872
Indiana	1871	Chicago	1873
Illinois	1872		
Texas	1874		

At the end of the third quarter of the nineteenth century there was a total of 188 public libraries in eleven states:[36]

Massachusetts	127
Illinois	14
New Hampshire	13
Ohio	9
Maine	8
Vermont	4
Connecticut	4
Wisconsin	4
Indiana	3
Iowa	1
Texas	1

Since the organization of public libraries presupposed an educated, or at least literate, adult public, it is not surprising that the development of libraries in the different states followed somewhat the same geographical pattern as that of the public schools established earlier.

Early Policies and Practices

The public librarians of the 1850's and 1860's were primarily scholarly men who had been recruited from educational and religious institutions and from university and social libraries. They were, for the most part, attracted to library work because of their interest in the content of books.

These men undertook the task of organizing public libraries with a definite concept of their function: to collect and preserve books that would contribute to personal development, moral betterment, and civic enlightenment. The collection and preservation of library books were primary concerns, while efforts directed toward the use of these books were secondary. The fulfillment of the librarian's duties, therefore, consisted of accumulating significant books, establishing policies to ensure their safety, and opening the library's doors to all adults who wished to consult the books.

Since the first task of these early years was to establish a basis for service, public librarians were occupied mainly with building book collections. With meager budgets and few staff assistants, they began to select the literature of intrinsic value: books covering various subjects and containing some positive contribution to knowledge. Their selection of books was governed by two major factors. First, these librarians were extremely conscious of their educational responsibilities. Second, most printing of full-length books at that period was limited to material important enough to be preserved.[37] Because of the specific educational responsibility of public libraries and the nature of the available books, most collections consisted of books that were either speculative or informative in content and erudite or literary in treatment.

Public librarians applied rigorous standards in the selection of books. Few compromises were made with popular taste. If fiction was included, it was usually only a small proportion of the total collection and was usually represented by such novelists as Dickens, Scott, Thackeray, Hawthorne, and Cooper. It was assumed that the collection of fiction would be limited to only those works of imaginative literature suitable for the family circle. There was no hesitation in excluding ephemeral or light reading. The trustees of the Boston Public Library made this point explicit:

> Notwithstanding many popular notions to the contrary, it is no part
> of the duty of a municipality to raise taxes for the amusement of the
> people. . . . the sole relation of a town library in the general interest is as
> a supplement to the school system; as an instrumentality of higher
> instruction to all classes of people.[38]

During the third quarter of the nineteenth century, public libraries were "storehouses of knowledge." The administrators of these newly formed civic agencies adopted the practices established earlier by the librarians of college, university, and social libraries. Like their precursors, they were primarily learned custodians, assuming intellectual and literary duties that were performed with an attitude of personal possessiveness toward the library's book collection. The public librarian, with his concern for the safety of the books and his desire to preserve them for future use, performed his task, in the opinion of James Russell Lowell, like "a watchdog," determined "to keep people as much as possible away from the books, and to hand them over to his successor as little worn by use as he could."[39]

Librarians constantly emphasized the importance of the rule that library books should be handled carefully and always treated with consideration. Since the books were often costly and difficult to replace, patrons were allowed only to consult them. The books were free to all but only for use in the building.[40] In discussing this practice, Melvil Dewey suggested that "the old librarian would have been as much shocked at the idea of taking a book from the building, as would the modern curator if an interested child should ask to carry home the bird of paradise."[41]

Attempts to stimulate the use of library books by making them easily accessible were of secondary importance. Few efforts were made to arrange books in such a way as to make them readily available to the user. Procedures and methods varied from library to library. There was no systematic or uniform plan of internal library organization. Each public library developed its own method of arranging and locating books on the shelves and its own procedures for maintaining a record of holdings.

Because of the composition of their book collections, public libraries were used primarily by those persons who had acquired competence in reading and knew what they wished to read. The library's clientele was made up of an intellectually superior minority of the adult population— persons of serious inclinations, such as the scholar, the man of cultivated tastes, and other bookish folk in the community. Because of their knowledge of books, they needed little in the way of personal suggestions or assistance from the librarian.

In summary, during the first period of public library development, librarians were in the process of establishing a structure for service. Because of the nature of their task, they were concerned principally with collecting books. They undertook this work with a clear understanding of the library's educational function—to make available books that would inform and enlighten. They implemented this objective by selecting books of intellectual and literary value and by making them available to all adults who wished to use them in the library building. Their efforts, representing years of arduous, intricate, and wearisome work, were to be appreciated more fully in the next period of public library expansion.

Organizing Resources

1876–1897

During the last quarter of the nineteenth century, the American public library attained a new level of maturity and set the direction for the course it has since followed. It was during this period that librarians developed technical processes which helped to bring about the efficient functioning of libraries. They removed many of the barriers which in the past had made libraries uninviting, and adopted practices that helped to make books more accessible within the library. They extended assistance to readers, provided additional services, and opened the doors of the library to a larger segment of the population. Thus, the storehouse type of public library and the custodian type of librarian was less prevalent as public libraries became freer and librarians became more service-conscious.

Founding of the American Library Association

One of the major events instrumental in strengthening the educational influence of public libraries occurred in 1876, when a group of university, college, government, and public librarians met in Philadelphia to form a national association for the purpose of discussing mutual problems. One hundred and three librarians registered as conferees, thirty of whom were from public libraries.[1] On the third day of the conference, October 6, 1876, a resolution was adopted that brought into existence the American Library Association. It read:

> For the purpose of promoting library interests of the country, and of
> increasing reciprocity of intelligence and good will among librarians and
> all interested in library economy and bibliographical studies, the

14

undersigned form themselves into a body to be known as the American Library Association.[2]

The organization of the American Library Association marked the beginning of an emerging library profession. Between 1876 and 1890, the leaders of the Association pioneered in developing methods for improving library services; described these methods in the pages of the *Library Journal,* the official publication of the Association; established criteria for raising library standards; and helped to make the name of librarian honored in places where the position previously had been held in low esteem.

Much of the early work of the Association was initiated by a relatively small number of administrators of free municipal libraries—men of unusual ability who, before the beginning of formal library training, were able to strike a balance between their knowledge of books, based on sound scholarship and classical learning, and their skill in organization, embodied in systematic procedures and operative experience. During the last quarter of the nineteenth century, these men provided the core of leadership for the newly formed Association.

Prominent among these library pioneers were men such as: Justin Winsor, Superintendent of the Boston Public Library and later Librarian of Harvard College; William Frederick Poole, Librarian of the Chicago Public Library; Charles Ammi Cutter, Librarian of the Forbes Library, Northampton, Massachusetts, and the master organizer who provided the foundation for the modern classification and cataloging system; Frederick Morgan Crunden, Librarian of the St. Louis Public Library; Samuel Swett Green, trustee and later Librarian of the Worcester (Massachusetts) Public Library; Henry Munson Utley, Secretary of the Detroit Public Library; John Cotton Dana, the forceful, outspoken, and brilliant promoter, who, after some experience in engineering and training in law, became Librarian of the Denver Public Library and later the Director of the Newark (New Jersey) Public Library; and William Howard Brett, who, after studying medicine and entering business as a bookseller, was appointed Librarian of the Cleveland Public Library and later became one of the foremost administrators and planners of public libraries.[3]

Between 1876 and 1897, each of these men served as president of the American Library Association: Winsor served for ten years; Poole and Cutter two years each; Crunden, Green, Utley, Dana, and Brett one year each. As the chief librarian of his institution, each contributed significant ideas and innovations which helped to advance American librarianship. As the elected leader of the Association, each helped stimulate librarians to consider possible directions for extending library services, examine methods of operation, and explore the practicality of adopting new policies.

At the first ALA Conference, public librarians began exploring three basic problems which continued to be discussed at the annual conferences and in the *Library Journal* during the next twenty years. These problems were: (1) the responsibility for extending and improving the educational work of the public library; (2) the desirability of including popular novels in the library's collection; and (3) the necessity of organizing library resources more efficiently. These discussions and the subsequent adoption of policies were of major importance in helping to create a tradition of service that differentiated the American public library of the 1880's and 1890's from its predecessor.

Educational Responsibility of the Public Library

Presidents of the American Library Association, other leaders in the profession, and laymen commented, between 1876 and 1897, on the library's educational responsibility, identifying the barriers which prevented librarians from performing this function more effectively and suggesting what the educational role of the library should be, the goals to be pursued, and the services to be provided in implementing these goals.

Educational Objective

Although the American Library Association did not issue an official statement of library objectives during this period, the inner circle of officers and leaders who guided the work of the Association and a number of prominent citizens who were instrumental in the establishment and growth of libraries were in agreement concerning the public library's educational responsibility. The following statements show the development and commonality of opinion relating to the educational objective of public libraries during these years:

> In 1876, Josiah P. Quincy, then a prominent Boston lawyer, stated that the public library was the "one secular institution which encourages self-development as an aim."[4]
> In 1876, Melvil Dewey, editor of the *Library Journal,* wrote:
>
> > The children of the lower classes have to commence work at a very early age, and it is impossible to keep them in the schools long enough to educate them to any degree. The school teaches them to read; the library must supply them with reading which shall serve to educate, and so it is that we are forced to divide popular education into two parts of almost equal importance and deserving equal attention: the free school and the free library.[5]
>
> In 1877, Charles Francis Adams, Jr., a trustee of the Quincy (Massachusetts) Public Library, maintained that the basic purpose of a public library was to serve as a means of continuing self-education.[6]

In 1879, Dr. William E. Foster, Librarian of the Providence (Rhode Island) Public Library, said that the library's end-in-view should be the development of the intellect.[7]

In 1884, Moses C. Tyler, Professor of American History at Cornell University, pointed out that the public library stood for the "wholesome truth that education is never finished and should not stop when one stops going to school."[8]

In 1885, James Russell Lowell, Professor of Literature at Harvard College and later editor of the *North American Review,* suggested that a "college education is an excellent thing; but, after all, the better part of every man's education is that which he gives himself, and it is for this that a good library should furnish the opportunity and the means."[9] And Frederic B. Perkins, Librarian of the San Francisco Public Library, stated that the most important function of a library was to supply books to those who wanted "to acquire or pursue an education . . ."[10]

In 1889, James M. Hubbard, assistant librarian of the Boston Public Library, reminded librarians that public libraries were established to promote the education and elevation of the people, "or, in other words, to make of it a People's High School. . . . The instruction, then, of the people was to be originally, and still ought to be, the chief object of the library."[11]

In 1891, Samuel Swett Green, Librarian of the Worcester (Massachusetts) Public Library, stated that the purpose of a library was to "stimulate and encourage persons of all ages, learned and unlearned, to make investigations and read good books."[12]

In 1894, Josephus N. Larned, Librarian of the Buffalo Library, suggested that the primary aim of a public library was to "serve as an agent of common culture."[13]

In 1895, Henry Munson Utley, Librarian of the Detroit Public Library, maintained that a "public library is purely and wholly educational, and for those persons forced to stop formal schooling to earn a living, it is truly the people's university."[14]

A composite statement of the library's educational responsibility, based on the above comments, would be: the educational objective of the public library is to provide the means by which adults—and especially those forced to leave school to earn a living—can continue their education.

Barriers to Effective Implementation

Although there was general consensus concerning the public library's educational objective, leaders of the profession realized that two barriers had to be overcome in the implementation of this objective. The barriers were: (1) the general public, as well as some librarians, did not view the public library as an educational agency, and (2) the public schools, which produced the potential users of a public library, did not perform their function as well as they should.

During the last quarter of the nineteenth century, library leaders realized that the public library, being a relatively new agency and offering an untried public service, was not equally appealing to everyone. Presidents of the American Library Association frequently reminded librarians of their responsibility to help strengthen the image of the public library as an educational agency and thereby raise their institution to the level of public favor enjoyed by the schools. These librarians, unlike the library pioneers of the 1850's and 1860's, did not accept the old rationalist belief that men had a yearning for culture and, given the means, would educate themselves.

The educational value of a public library, wrote Melvil Dewey, was not "universally granted," because librarians had been unable to find a way to demonstrate that value to the general public.[15] And the editors of the U.S. Bureau of Education's special report on public libraries pointed out, in 1876, that the influence of "the librarian as an educator is rarely estimated by outside observers, and probably seldom fully realized even by himself."[16]

There was confusion and, in some cases, lack of understanding and conviction among librarians concerning the educational responsibility of libraries. The result was that the general public thought of the public library as a junior partner in the local educational enterprise. Henry Munson Utley stressed the seriousness of the situation. The public library, he said, was not "a public charity . . . there is no duty of kindness or good-will which requires the furnishing of reading matter for the use of the community. . . . The only basis on which the expense of public libraries can be justified is that their purpose is educational."[17]

Three major approaches to the problem of strengthening the image of the public library as an educational agency were suggested: (1) improving the methodology of libraries; (2) developing, among other educators, recognition of the library as an educational agency; and (3) presenting a factual picture of the work of the library to the general public. Melvil Dewey, in attempting to motivate librarians to spend more time in improving the methodology of the public library, concluded that

> . . . if the best methods can be applied by the best librarians, the public
> may soon be brought to recognize our claim that the free library
> ranks with the free school. We hold that there is no work reaching
> further in its influence and deserving more honor than the work which
> a competent and earnest librarian can do for his community.
>
> . . . .
> The time was when a library was very like a museum, and a librarian

was a mouser in musty books, and visitors looked with curious eyes at ancient tomes and manuscripts. The time is when the library is a school, and the librarian is in the highest sense a teacher, and the visitor is a reader among the books as a workman among his tools.[18]

The second approach stressed that, if libraries were to be viewed as educational agencies, recognition would have to come first from other educators, particularly those associated with public education. Since a multitude of readers "find in the public libraries their only means of intellectual improvement," wrote the editors of the U.S. Bureau of Education's special report on libraries,

> educators should be able to know the direction and gauge the extent and results of this potential influence, and . . . librarians should not only understand their primary duties as purveyors of literary supplies to the people, but also realize their high privileges and responsibilities as teachers. . . .[19]

The third, and perhaps most important, approach consisted of presenting a factual picture of the library to the public. "This great work we can, as librarians, promote not only by bringing the work of the library to the highest possible state of efficiency, but also by taking all proper means of calling attention to its value, and letting its good work be known."[20] In order to create a more desirable image of the public library as as educational agency, librarians were encouraged to think of the library "as an essential part" of the educational system,[21] to understand their "high privileges and responsibilities as teachers,"[22] and to create among the general population a conception of the public library as "the people's university."[23]

If the public library was unable to achieve fully its educational objective, one of the barriers, in the opinion of some librarians and laymen, was that the public schools did not perform their function as effectively as they should. The problem was stated by Melvil Dewey:

> We begin to see that the utmost that we can hope for the masses is schooling til they can take the author's meaning from the printed page. I do not mean merely to pronounce the words or pass the tests for illiteracy, but to understand. Observation has convinst me that the reason why so many peopl ar not habitual readers is, in most cases, they never really learnd to read; and startling as this may seem, tests wil show that many a man who would resent the charge of illiteracy is wholly unabl to reproduce the author's tho'ts by looking at the printed page.[24]

Librarians, and leading citizens interested in library development, attributed the problem to various causes. The public schools tried to cover too much; the old system, said James Russell Lowell, which taught merely "the three R's, and taught them well, was the better."[25] The schools, it was maintained, did not teach children how to read; they only taught the mechanical part of reading.[26] As for methods of instruction, Josiah P. Quincy suggested that when good books could be obtained only by the wealthy, there was "some excuse for crowding a child's memory with disconnected scraps of knowledge. But now that the free library is opened, sounder methods are demanded."[27] And Dr. William E. Foster, Librarian of the Providence (Rhode Island) Public Library, believed that the methods of the public schools should

> ... aim to bring the strong light of interest to bear on the presentation
> of each subject, and must be essentially direct and personal, and
> must follow up the first steps by continuous efforts. Instead of a policy
> which contemplates brilliant but superficial operations, should be chosen
> one which, with patience and persistency, enters upon measures which
> require time for their development, but whose results are
> substantial and permanent.[28]

Although various causes of the deficiency of the schools were suggested, the leading librarians agreed on a single standard by which the work of the public school should be measured. The ultimate purpose of the school should be "to prepare the children of the community for the far greater work of educating themselves."[29] And the success of the school, said Josephus N. Larned, should be determined not by the

> ... little portion of actual learning which its students take out of it,
> but by the persisting strength of the impulses to know and to think which
> they carry from the school into their later lives.[30]

The basis of this reasoning was that the work of the classical schools, serving a small and select class, was to prepare students for college. The work of the public schools, serving the majority, was to fit students "for the people's college, the town library,"[31] which depended upon the individual student's being able to read effectively. This competence was the important connecting link between school education and self-education, the bridge, so to speak, leading from the public school to the public library. Librarians, therefore, attempted to point out some of the limitations of the schools without alienating school officials. They realized that they must have the support and cooperation of the schools in order to carry out the library's educational role.

Educational Role

During the latter half of the 1870's and the early part of the 1880's, the educational role of the public library was to supplement the work of the public schools. Then, about 1885, library leaders began to seek a more substantial role for the library. No longer content to have the library serve as an appendage to the system of public education, librarians took steps to create a more influential role for the library as an educational agency. Thus, the conception of the library's role was broadened to include the idea that the public library was not to *supplement* but to *complement* the work of the public school.

The line of reasoning used to support the claim that the public library was a complementary educational force was that the public library and the public school both aimed to increase personal understanding and to provide opportunities for culture. The public school, working with groups of students, initiated the educational process; the public library, working with individuals, continued the process throughout life. The school and the library were, said Dr. William E. Foster, "complements of each other, two halves of one complete purpose, neither in itself possessing every requisite advantage, but, taken in connection, lacking nothing, whether universality, systematic methods, directness, adaption to individuality, or durability of impressions."[32] Each of these institutions, it was claimed, was inadequate without the other. The schools, wrote Melvil Dewey, "give the chisel; the libraries the marble; there can be no statues without both."[33]

Educational Services

Another reason for broadening the library's educational role was the nature and scope of the educational services being provided by libraries. Between 1876 and 1897, the educational services consisted of making available books of educational value and of providing assistance to readers. These services were directed toward three major goals: personal development, moral improvement, and civic enlightenment.[34]

The majority of public libraries of this period carried out their educational responsibility by making available a collection of books of educational value. Most library collections were composed of works of instruction for personal development and civic enlightenment, moral and religious books to help combat inebriety and crime, and imaginative literature for mental and physical relaxation. Although some concessions were made to popular taste, most public libraries obtained the best books available in order to establish what were beginning to be called "well-rounded collections." In contrast to the earlier period of library development (1833–1875), the public librarians of the 1880's and 1890's provided readers with a larger and more varied selection of books, and, in a few libraries, attempts were being made to assist readers.

A small number of librarians pioneered during this period in establishing practices to make libraries more useful. In 1876, when the majority of librarians maintained that personal assistance to readers was beyond the province of their duties, William I. Fletcher, Librarian of the Watkinson Library of Hartford, Connecticut, stated that "where there is leisure for it, applicants for books should receive the best assistance the attendants can render in the form of information not furnished by the catalogues, or general aids in making selections." Fletcher also suggested that the chief librarian should frequently be available at the circulation desk. He predicted that the librarian who withdrew to the "seclusion of a private office" would never be able to interest the public in the library or in its intelligent use.[85]

The first detailed description of a program of personal assistance to individual readers was made by Samuel Swett Green in a paper read at the 1876 conference of librarians.[36] Green proposed that librarians should do more than merely make available catalogs and other aids for readers; they should extend a cordial reception to readers and give personal attention to their reading needs. He suggested various ways in which librarians could help patrons find the materials best suited to their capacities, and pointed out that "there are few pleasures comparable to that of associating with curious and vigorous young minds, and of aiding them in realizing their ideals."[37] By providing such assistance, Green concluded, the librarian could make his institution a forceful instrument for popular education. Green's paper, which later appeared as an article in the *Library Journal,* had much influence; so persuasive was its message that it was noticed and commended in the *Boston Daily Advertiser* and later in the *New York World,* which complained of the unaccommodating spirit in the libraries of that city.[38]

The practice of assisting readers became more widely accepted by librarians during the 1880's. At the Lake George ALA Conference in 1885, Bradford K. Pierce, Librarian of the Free Library at Newton, Massachusetts, stated that libraries were becoming "powerful elements of culture." The reason for this extension of the library's influence, suggested Pierce, was that

> . . . superintendents and librarians do not simply remain at their desks,
> or stand behind their tables to respond to the call for books, but make
> themselves felt in the community, aiding in the investigations of students,
> assisting in the search for authorities, facts, and illustrations, suggesting
> plans for interesting the youthful readers in scientific or literary studies,
> and calling attention to the rich accumulations upon the library shelves.[39]

The following year, Frederick M. Crunden, Librarian of the St. Louis Public Library, reported on his study of "aids to readers," based on data collected from 108 libraries. He found a growing interest among librarians concerning the provision of personal assistance:

> Among the most acceptable and effective methods for assisting readers to
> the best books and sources of information, fifty-three librarians report
> "personal help." Many of them believe this to be the most important of
> all "aids," and on this point again your reporter is glad to record his vote
> with the majority. His own opinion is entirely in accord with the sentiment
> expressed in a number of the reports, that nothing can take the place
> of "an intelligent and obliging assistant at the desk."[40]

Although the majority of librarians who participated in the survey reported that personal assistance was the most effective method for aiding readers, they emphasized that librarians with special skills were needed to provide this service. In 1889, Charles A. Cutter, Librarian of the Forbes Library (Northampton, Massachusetts) and then President of the American Library Association, suggested that when there were several librarians at the circulation desk, one at least should be competent to advise readers. But if there were only one librarian, he should be chosen because he had some knowledge of books and human nature. "Let no one imagine," said Cutter, "that this attendant—whom in library matters we might call the Adviser or Suggester—will have an easy time, or that a successful adviser can be found everywhere."[41]

During the 1890's, the provision of personal assistance to readers increased, and the educational value of this service was stressed. Dr. Lewis H. Steiner, Librarian of the Enoch Pratt Free Library (Baltimore, Maryland), predicted that the public library of the future

> ... will not only be a warehouse of books, where the most complete adaptation of the best technical methods for their arrangement, classification, and management shall be employed, but a realization of a people's university, supplied with instructors—whatever names be given them—fully competent to guide and instruct its pupils, and to make its books of incalculable value; over all of which will preside the one mind that is full of sympathy with its students, and, at the same time, broad enough and wise enough to comprehend all necessary practical details, while it commits these to subordinate officers—some to manage those of a mere technical character, and others to exercise those instructional duties that are demanded in order to make the library most useful to the greatest number.[42]

As the number of libraries providing personal assistance to readers increased, attempts were made to encourage librarians to improve the quality of this service. William Howard Brett, Librarian of the Cleveland Public Library, in his presidential address at the 1897 ALA Conference, stated that the personal influence of librarians who assisted and advised readers was the most potent factor in molding community reading. These librarians, he said, made the library a teaching force rather than a mere storehouse. The value and propriety of their work were unquestionable. Therefore, all efforts should be made, suggested Brett, to find means of furthering their work and of increasing their efficiency.[43]

Librarians' willingness to provide assistance to readers in locating and selecting books came about gradually. At first only a few librarians experimented in assisting readers; this was followed by considerable discussion concerning the desirability of providing this service; then, when the need was more fully recognized, more librarians began assisting readers, and, by 1890, attempts were being made to extend the provision and improve the quality of this service. With the growing concern over the library's role as an educational institution, this service was gradually accepted not as peripheral but as one of the library's main responsibilities.

Two major factors influenced the growth and implementation of the educational services of public libraries during these years: (1) increases in the educational level of the population due to compulsory attendance laws in thirty-two of the states and to the gradual extension of the public school system, and (2) improvements in printing and increased book production and the subsequent growth of library collections.

The librarians of this period, unlike their predecessors, were more concerned with the organization and utilization of library books than with their preservation. They were desirous of establishing personal contact with readers, making books productive, and serving a wider group of readers. In short, public librarians were becoming service-oriented. They were attempting to relate the library to the interests of more people in the population. With this intent they added, to duties already engrossing, two additional services.

Emergence of Other Objectives

Recreational Objective

No issue of the 1870's and 1880's caused librarians greater concern than whether to include popular novels in the library's collection. The controversy, however, was not about the admission of clearly inferior or sensational fiction[44] but about the addition of popular works by such novelists as Trollope, Twain, and Du Maurier. Some librarians held the view that the inclusion of popular novels in the library's collection was a means of attracting a larger clientele, elevating reading tastes, and providing wholesome recreation, while others maintained that popular novels should not be provided at public expense.

The first reason put forward by librarians who advocated the inclusion of popular fiction was that public libraries could attract a larger number of patrons by leveling off their standards to the desires and interests of a wider circle than that embracing learners alone. They asserted that publicly supported libraries should not be stocked with books that the majority of the people did not read; instead, libraries should contain books adapted to the wants of the masses who bore the burden of taxation. "The people do not demand vicious literature," said Samuel Swett Green, "but they do demand exciting stories; and neither citizens nor city government will support a library generously that does not contain the books they and their families want."[45] Since the majority of citizens did not use the library, it was argued that librarians should adopt a more democratic and practical policy in order to give more potential users the books they liked and could understand.

The second reason supporting the argument that popular novels should be supplied by libraries was that they were a means of gradually elevating the reading tastes of the uncultivated masses. "We must interest the reader," wrote William Frederick Poole, "before we can educate him; and, to this end, must commence at his own standard of intelligence."[46] This approach consisted of attracting potential readers by providing the "pleasant literature of the day" and implanting in them a taste for reading. To lure the untrained reader to the library, suggested William I. Fletcher, librarians should follow the old recipe for cooking a hare, which began, "First catch your hare."[47] Once this group of readers were in the habit of using the library, it was assumed that they could by easy stages and with the assistance of the librarian be introduced to higher levels of reading. The way to elevate the reading taste of the public, it was suggested, was not by neglect but by sympathy and a purposive program of assistance; not by refusing to provide the books the masses wanted to read but by beginning with the books they were interested in and, through encouragement and guidance, helping them in their choice of books to graduate to more substantive reading.

In comparing the two uses of fiction—to attract a larger clientele and to elevate reading taste—William E. Foster said:

> The one attempts only to supply the public with what it wants; the other,
> striving after the truest improvement of the readers, in time secures,
> with the growth of intelligent appreciation, an interest even more active
> and vastly more permanent than the other. No library may safely disregard
> either class of methods, and their proper adjustment is a point which
> may very profitably engage much of the librarian's attention.[48]

The third reason given in support of supplying popular novels—and the major justification for the provision of these materials—was that a need was evident for an increase in recreation as a part of adult life and few recreational facilities were available for the general public. Novel reading, it was pointed out, was a rational and wholesome form of recreation. It afforded mental relaxation to the working man who was subjected to monotonous labor day after day. On the authority of the psychologist G. Stanley Hall, librarians could claim that a good novel rested the nerves in a more wholesome way "than does a cup of strong tea," and to this they added, "Certainly more wholesome than some of the other stimulating drinks and activities resorted to by urban industrial workers."[49] Since a pleasant novel helped to add new dimensions to living, to open up new areas of interest, and to make life more meaningful, public libraries could, by providing imaginative and popular reading, provide a needed and significant service.

This view, however, was not shared by all librarians. Those who were in favor of excluding popular novels from public libraries argued that it was not the duty of a municipality to raise taxes to be used for the amusement of the people. Circulating (rental) libraries provided amusement, and public libraries provided education. Therefore, public libraries that stocked popular fiction, said Charles Francis Adams, Jr., were invading the sphere of the circulating library; and, in doing so, not only were "removing a very desirable as well as natural check on an excessive indulgence in one form of amusement, but are doing it through a misapplication of public money."[50] It was also claimed that novels gave false ideas of life and made the masses dissatisfied with their "lowly but honest occupations,"[51] and that, in some instances, insanity was brought about by overindulgence in novel reading.[52]

The librarians who rallied against the inclusion of popular novels maintained that they were not servants to supply a demand but were responsible for the direction of a new and mighty force for enlightenment—"a central beacon from whence the rays of light shall stream into every home."[53] They hoped that the group of librarians who were concerned with furnishing amusement would "gradually attain conceptions of public duty which will prevent them from courting a temporary popularity by hastening to supply immature and unregulated minds with the feverish excitements which they have learned to crave."[54]

The majority of public librarians, however, took a more moderate view toward the provision of novels. They proposed that libraries should not respond to every demand but should be responsive to reasonable requests. Fiction should be kept to a minimum, and discretion should be used in its selection so as to secure only the best.[55] The problem, said Frank P. Hill, Librarian of the Newark Public Library, was in deciding where to draw the line. "I am not one to believe," he said,

> that everything asked for by the public should be supplied. A public
> library supported by municipal tax must, to a certain extent, respond to
> the demand of the public. At the same time, the educational work should
> ever be considered the most important. . . . It is all very well to talk of
> educating the people, but if they refuse to be educated, what is to be done
> about it? We can only try to lead the people to a higher and better course.
> It is the duty of the librarian to assist and guide the reader, and he can
> be of service to the novel reader, as well as the searcher after knowledge.[56]

The controversy about the provision of popular novels marked the beginning of the conflict between the library's two prinicipal objectives: education and recreation. This conflict, which is still of concern today, was based on a questionable assumption. It was assumed, primarily because of the way book collections were organized in libraries, that there was a clear differentiation between two kinds of books—fiction and nonfiction—with fiction being associated with recreation and nonfiction with education. This categorization, however, failed to take into account two factors. First, not all fiction is recreational; some is obviously of higher educational value than some nonfiction. And not all nonfiction is educational; many works in this category, consisting of friendly tips and helpful hints, do not represent a contribution to knowledge or understanding of permanent worth. Second, the purposes of readers, their educational level, and their reading abilities must be taken into consideration. To paraphrase an old adage, one man's recreation is another man's education. And, conversely, one man's education is another man's recreation.

The historic conflict between the recreational and the educational objectives, presented in terms of fiction versus nonfiction, has brought forth little understanding. The dividing line between what is educational and what is recreational in libraries cannot be determined, in the judgment of the writer, until much more is known about the reasons why readers use the library and the distinctions between two kinds of books: those which aid various types of readers to gain understanding and those which do not.

Between 1876 and 1897, public librarians did become more aware of their responsibility to furnish reading for a larger section of the population. In order to encourage library use, some concessions to popular taste were made. Nevertheless, the majority of librarians, who were predominantly men of learning and scholarly attainments, adhered to the canons of good taste in the selection of books. Popular novels, such as *Tom Sawyer, Ben Hur, Trilby,* and *Little Lord Fauntleroy,* were provided. Although the surrender to fiction was only partial during this period, librarians recognized that the public library no longer existed exclusively for *one* function.

Reference Objective

As library collections increased in size, indexes and guides were developed as a means of making more effective use of resources. With the use of these aids librarians began, during the 1880's, to provide an additional service which consisted of answering questions, locating facts, and directing patrons to books that could be consulted in answering inquiries. This service, which acquired the name of "reference work," was distinct from personal assistance to readers in that the former was concerned with the supplying of information and sources of information, and the latter with helping patrons locate and select books.

To facilitate informational reference service, urban libraries began, during the 1890's, to organize special reference collections, consisting of dictionaries, encyclopedias, maps, government reports, and other materials which could be consulted in providing brief answers to various kinds of questions. As these libraries increased in size, informational reference service was provided by a separate library department and required the full-time efforts of one or more staff members.[57]

Near the end of the nineteenth century, the provision of recreational

reading and informational reference service had begun to make more
and more demands on the librarian's time, and confusion was developing as to which of the library's three objectives—education, recreation,
or reference—was primary. Herbert Putnam, Librarian of the Boston
Public Library, in his presidential address at the 1898 ALA Conference,
said:

> Like the strong man in the circus, we have been taking on one activity
> after another until we have become a great aggregate of hitherto unrelated
> activities. For him to win applause it is sufficient to support these on his
> own foundations and retain his equilibrium. But we are not content
> to stand at rest. And our anxious problem must be to bear this great
> mass and still move forward.[58]

Librarians' eagerness to reach a wider audience had led to the extension of services and the growth of book collections. Impelled by their
desire to make books useful, librarians now devoted increasing attention to the needs of their clientele, and their concern for the reader led
not only to the provision of additional services but also to the development of new bibliographical aids.

Increasing Effectiveness

The librarians of this period directed a major portion of their efforts
toward organizing library resources and developing procedures to facilitate their use. Technical processes were devised and operational policies
adopted that established the pattern of modern library practice.

Technical Processes

The welcoming speaker at the 1876 ALA Conference warned librarians
to adopt some form of science in their work lest they be buried in the
mass of books they were handling.[59] Advances in printing had increased
substantially the number of book titles being published, library book
collections had grown rapidly, and librarians needed more efficient means
of knowing what books a library contained and establishing a system
for making them easily accessible. Between 1876 and 1885, librarians
concentrated on developing effective methods for arranging and locating books on the library shelves. Much arduous work went into the
construction of catalogs, classification systems, shelving arrangements,
and numerous technical devices designed to improve library operations.
And so librarians, preoccupied with manipulative procedures and processes, gradually became technicians as well as bookmen.

Many of the modern features of library organization were developed
during this period. Major contributions included: Charles A. Cutter's
Rules for a Printed Dictionary Catalogue, which formed the basis for
all future ALA cataloging codes, and the *A.L.A. Catalog Rules: Author*

and Title Entries, which set the trend of dictionary arrangements for library catalogs; and Melvil Dewey's *The Decimal Classification and Relative Index,* first published in 1876. The development of these and other library tools helped to make books physically accessible within the library in the most economical and expedient manner.

Operational Policies

A gradual but significant change in the operational policies of public libraries occurred during the 1880's and 1890's. New library policies, designed to remove restrictions on the use of library materials, included: the circulation of books for home reading, thus permitting patrons to use books at home instead of confining such use to the library building;[60] open shelves, which allowed readers to see and handle library books instead of being restricted to a catalog;[61] Sunday opening, which became a generally accepted practice around 1890;[62] and increased hours of opening, which enabled the laboring classes to make fuller use of the library.[63] The adoption of each of these policies was a step forward in extending and encouraging library use.

Community-centered Libraries

To bring the library into closer contact with the community, three major services were added during the 1880's and 1890's: personal assistance to readers, recreational reading, and informational reference service. The provision of these services was an attempt to meet the reasonable expectations of readers and to open up new avenues of communication between the library and the public. One of the most important steps in this direction was the development of multipurpose book collections. The day of the standard library collection, consisting exclusively of erudite and literary works, was almost over. More librarians were recognizing, as Justin Winsor said, that "there can be no such thing as a model collection so long as communities differ and individuality survives."[64]

By 1897, American public libraries had become firmly established as community institutions, presided over by librarians who were intent on providing library services to all classes of people. Along with their desire to improve services, librarians devised methods of recording and indexing library resources and instituted policies that helped to make books more accessible within the library. The development of technical processes effected a systematic library organization, provided a body of knowledge relating to library procedures, and left librarians much freer than formerly for the extension of services.

A definite trend toward better service was characterized by librarians' concern for individual readers, and by their desire to clarify the library's role in encouraging self-education among the adults of the community.

Pointing out that the library was an informal educational institution, librarians stressed that their approach focused on self-education in an atmosphere of freedom, while the emphasis of the public school was on the transmission of knowledge in an atmosphere of restraint or discipline. The library and the school complemented each other, and the virtue of each was that it was not the other. Librarians believed that the educational services of public libraries should be developed along library lines, and any attempt to emulate school practices would impair the effectiveness of these services.

In carrying out their educational responsibilities, librarians were concerned not only with supplying books but with assisting adults who wished to continue their education. In an effort to strengthen the educational influence of the library, librarians defined more sharply the library's educational objective and role; called attention to the distinctive features of the educational method of the library; and contributed, more than any group of librarians since, to a conception of the library as a community institution for self-education.

Library Pioneers

Many of the advances in library development during the 1880's and 1890's came about as the result of the work of the American Library Association, under the leadership of such library pioneers as Justin Winsor, William Frederick Poole, Charles A. Cutter, Melvil Dewey, William I. Fletcher, and Henry M. Utley. In 1897, William H. Brett said:

> It is not too much to say that during all these years no important advance has been made in library plans, nor any valuable improvement in library methods and appliances, which was not first proposed by a member of the Association and discussed at its meetings, or in the pages of the *Journal*.[65]

Indeed, much of the professional knowledge of librarians today is due to the work of the pioneer technicians and innovators of the 1880's and 1890's. The contributions of later years have but filled in the outlines drawn at that time. The advances in librarianship that have come about during the last seventy years have broadened but not altered fundamentally the framework of the public library which the early leaders had fashioned by 1890.

Chapter

III

Extending Services

1898–1919

During the first two decades of the twentieth century, librarians under-took a vast program of extension, which was designed to bring library services to a much larger proportion of the population. As a result of these efforts in extending services and in making them as attractive to the public as possible, the public library was well on its way to becoming a more permanent part of the American scene.

Book Promotion

Public libraries changed in an almost revolutionary manner between the turn of the century and the beginning of World War I. By 1900, the problems of processing and organizing books had been partially solved. Then, librarians—some of whom had received training in library schools—directed their energies toward locating a larger market for their services. With the intent of "bringing to all the people the books that belong to them," librarians utilized methods to increase the use and geographic coverage of public libraries. They advertised the library's services. They invited people of all social and economic classes to use the library. They increased the size of the library's clientele by providing books and services for children, and attracted a larger number of adult readers by increasing the library's stock of popular novels. Next, they went outside the library. They established branch libraries in locations which would be accessible to the greatest number of readers, and they took books to rural people by means of wagons and trucks. These efforts marked the beginning of a new phase of development, with major emphasis on library extension work, service to children, and other means of increasing library usage.

Library Extension

About 1900, some librarians began to suggest that, because of the rapid growth of cities, many urban libraries were located too far from the mass of people to be of the greatest use. In persuading city officials of the need to make libraries more accessible, librarians asserted that public libraries should be "scattered through the community as much as schools. You say that the child must not be required to walk too far to school. The same condition is true of our public libraries."[1] Motivated by the belief that they should facilitate the efforts of readers to obtain books, librarians in large cities established subsidiary centers of distribution: delivery stations, where books could be ordered from the main library and through which they could be returned but where no permanent collection was kept; deposit stations, where small collections of books were sent from the main library to be circulated freely and then returned as a whole for a new collection; and branch libraries, containing permanent collections of books and providing all the services of a small library.

Not until libraries were firmly established in the majority of cities and towns of the nation did library service to rural communities have a beginning. The first attempt to provide books for people in very small villages or on farms was undertaken by state library agencies[2] through a system of traveling libraries. Small collections of books, packed in boxes for transportation by freight or mule back, were sent to rural areas and placed in postoffices, stores, or homes.[3] In some sections of the country, however, particularly in the vast rural areas of the South and the West, traveling libraries were ineffective. Therefore, in attempting to make books more accessible and to ensure continuing financial support for rural library services, the proponents of library extension turned to the county as the basis for library organization.

The most significant phase of library extension began in 1898, when the first county library was established in Washington County, Maryland. Service was provided to the residents of the county through traveling libraries, deposit stations, and an innovation called the "book wagon," which was the forerunner of the bookmobile. In order to reach the more remote sections of Washington County, a covered wagon— fitted with shelves containing about two hundred books, pulled by a horse, and operated by Miss Mary L. Titcomb of Hagerstown, Maryland—was sent out on its first trip in 1905.[4]

Between 1900 and 1910, Wisconsin, Oregon, and Minnesota provided for county support of library service, but development was irregular and slow until California started a vigorous campaign in 1911 to organize county libraries on a statewide basis. By 1916, county libraries were established in thirty-seven of California's fifty-nine counties.[5] During the next two decades, outstanding county library systems were developed in Louisiana, New Jersey, Ohio, and North Carolina. Several technological developments of this period, such as the widespread use of the automobile and the telephone, were instrumental in the extension of services. Perhaps even more important in terms of adult reading was the electrification of urban areas which resulted in making home reading a more congenial activity.

Service to Children

Prior to 1890, when the emphasis of public libraries was on the provision of adult services, many libraries had signs which read: "Children and dogs not admitted."[6] As child labor became illegal, as the number of public schools increased, and a higher literacy of the population was achieved, public libraries began to extend privileges to children. At first, only a few libraries provided this service. Then, around the turn of the century, service to children became generally accepted, separate children's rooms were established, and a training school for children's librarians was organized at the Carnegie Library of Pittsburgh.

Library service to children was first provided to help train the adult readers of the future. Dr. Edward A. Birge, Dean of the College of Letters and Science at the University of Wisconsin and Director of the Madison (Wisconsin) Free Library, emphasized that the purpose of library work with children was to develop in the youth of the nation "a voluntary association with books which lie wholly outside the school program." It aimed, he said,

> to begin the early formation of the habit of reading as distinguished
> from study—a habit which will be permanent, instead of ending with the
> period of formal education. It recognizes the fact that school life
> must soon end, and that when the end comes, the important feature of
> the child's intellectual condition is not so much the amount he has learned
> as the temper and habit of his mind toward books.[7]

During the first two decades of the twentieth century, service to children became a major activity of public libraries of all sizes. Henry M. Utley stated, in 1911, that one of the most important and desirable developments in library extension was in the area of work with children. "Twenty years ago," he said, "there was not such a thing as a children's room in a public library. Now there is scarcely a library which has not such a room set apart distinctively for children."[8] Later, children's rooms were organized into departments. Service to children soon became popular with the public and, about 1915, it accounted for a third or more of the entire book circulation in many libraries.

Increasing Library Usage

In this same period librarians—assuming that institutions which endured were those which kept in touch with the people, responded to public demand, and changed their policies accordingly—adopted a philosophy of service directed toward the ideal of finding a reader for every book on the library shelves and providing a book for every reader in the community. To accomplish these ends, they began to utilize publicity techniques that had made other enterprises successful, to acquire an increasing number of popular novels, and to adopt methods for disseminating library books to people in all parts of the community. These activities were effective in increasing library use. They produced larger and larger circulation figures, and librarians gradually began to measure the value of their work in quantitative terms.

In extending services, librarians increased the public library's circle of influence. No longer serving only the educated or learned classes, librarians became more responsive in supplying the reading wants of patrons, more democratic in their attitude toward serving the general public, and more confident of their ability to make the public library a "popular" institution. Concurrent with the emphasis on library extension was the impetus given to the establishment of new libraries.

Andrew Carnegie and Library Expansion

One of the major influences on the development of the American public library movement was the vast library expansion that came about during this period as the result of the benevolence of Andrew Carnegie, the millionaire ironmaster. Carnegie gave more than $41 million for the erection of 1,679 public library buildings, located in 1,408 localities in the United States.[9]

In deciding on public libraries as the major concern of his philanthropy, Carnegie stated that, in addition to his youthful impressions of a lending library,[10] his chief reason for "selecting public libraries [was] my belief, as Carlyle has recorded, that the true university of these days is a collection of books, and that thus such libraries are entitled to a first place as instruments for the elevation of the masses of the people."[11] He attempted, through the provision of library facilities, to extend free access to books—a condition which, he proposed, would eventually lead to a gradual raising of mass intelligence. Burton J. Hendrick, the author of a definitive biography of Carnegie, wrote:

> The greatest single obstruction to progress, in his [Carnegie's] opinion,
> was ignorance. Human kind advances in one effective way, by the
> dissemination of ideas. Poor man struggles forward, encumbered by a
> mass of rubbish, the prejudices, superstitions, animosities, impossible
> loyalties and irrational preconceptions that are the heritage of a primitive

past; not until this growth is cleared away and inherent reason is permitted
to assert its supremacy will anything resembling real civilization
be attained. The world is a mass of evils, for which there is ultimately
only one cure: the development of a new mentality in place of the old.[12]

Carnegie was convinced that of all benevolences the public library was
the most significant, because it gave nothing without demanding something in return and helped only those who were willing to help themselves.

In all of his offers to communities concerning the erection of public
library buildings, Carnegie set forth one prerequisite—the recipient
community, before receiving the gift, was required to pass an ordinance
guaranteeing from tax sources an annual amount for library support
equal to one tenth of the gift.[13] Because of this stipulation, what is often
remembered about Carnegie is not his belief in the educational value of
public libraries, but his economic philosophy concerning the means for
the continued support of the libraries made possible by his gifts. "I do
not wish to be remembered," he once said, "for what I have given, but
for what I have persuaded others to give."[14] Carnegie, wrote Hendrick,

. . . sometimes referred to his library structures as "bribes." By dangling
before the popular eye a neat and commodious building he tempted the
authorities to do their duty. His "deal" with mayors, boards of aldermen
and the like afforded him a kind of canny pleasure, for America's
conscript fathers, stolid and balky in the face of growing public opinion,
suddenly found that Carnegie, by proposing so palpable an argument
as money on the popular side, had lighted fires beneath them. His gift of
$5,200,000 to the city of New York for branch libraries brought
a flood of felicitations. "Don't congratulate me," he said to a friend. "It's
the best bargain I ever made. The money I have given is a small affair.
See what I have compelled the city of New York to give!"—for the
metropolis, in accepting this offer, had promised an annual and
permanent appropriation of more than $500,000. On this point of making
the taxpayers assume maintenance Carnegie was inflexible. To it no
exception was made. . . .[15]

Carnegie never gave funds for purchasing library books or for the
operation of public libraries. He gave money only for the erection of
public library buildings. The ownership, control, administration, and
support of the public libraries made possible by his gifts were always
the responsibility of the communities in which the buildings were located.

In 1911, the Carnegie Corporation was established to continue the
further administration of Carnegie's philanthropic enterprises. In 1917,
the Carnegie Corporation discontinued the practice of making grants
for the erection of library buildings and began to allocate funds to be
used for scholarships to library school students, financial aid to library
schools, and research to strengthen librarianship.

Andrew Carnegie saw in the public library the means by which ordinary men and women could lift themselves to higher levels of culture and achievement. With this purpose he began his library benefactions, which eventually resulted in almost doubling the number of American communities served by public libraries. Moreover, the Carnegie grants stimulated library endowments and library appropriations. In helping to spread the idea of the free library as an essential public institution, it is unlikely that any other person has made as enduring a contribution as that of Andrew Carnegie. With the great increase in the number of public libraries, together with the desire on the part of librarians to make these newly established institutions as attractive to the public as possible, there arose a new conception of the library's aims and responsibilities, which resulted in more attention being given to the provision of recreational and informational services.

Recreational and Informational Services

Recreational Service

The discussion of education versus recreation, which began during the late 1870's, was continued—but along different lines—by the librarians of the early 1900's. Whereas the librarians of the earlier period (1876–1897) discussed the desirability of including popular fiction in the library's collection, the librarians of this period (1898–1919) debated about *how much* popular fiction should be supplied.

Recreational reading through libraries was fully recognized during this period by both librarians and library users. Librarians, considering popular demand to be the logical criterion for effective service, supplied[16] and circulated[17] more current fiction. By providing library users with more of the books they wanted to read, librarians increased circulation. Then, they began to point out that more extensive use of the public library was proof that it was truly a democratic institution which provided reading for all classes of people. No longer serving as mediators between the great unwashed audience and the unvarnished truth of books, public librarians became promoters and purveyors of library resources.

Although the majority of public librarians did not purchase dime novels and the much-advertised sensational fiction of the day,[18] they did supply the public with generous quantities of current fiction, and at times they were criticized for this practice. In defense, librarians responded with two arguments. One stated that it was the duty of public libraries to provide books that were "merely recreational"—books that helped individuals to pass time pleasantly—because they promoted personal happiness and social well-being. This point of view was fostered and sanctioned to some extent by the development, during the early

1900's, of the organized recreational movement in the United States, which began with the recognition of the fact that the urban environment offered no adequate outlet for the wholesome energies of both children and adults. Dr. Edward A. Birge, in addressing a group of librarians in 1905, said:

> We cannot remind ourselves too frequently that the fundamental purpose
> of good books and so of the library which possesses them, is to give
> pleasure, and that the library ought to be more closely associated with
> pleasure than any other institution supported by the public.[19]

It was also suggested that popular novels provided many library users with an innocent and praiseworthy form of entertainment.

The second argument asserted that it was the duty of public libraries to provide "recreational" books—books that helped to foster human development—because they promoted the healthy and intelligent use of the faculties, and they often assisted individuals in the achievement of emotional stability, in the development of better spoken and written language, and in the attainment of social skills. John Shaw Billings, Director of the New York (City) Public Library, told the members of the National Municipal League in 1903 that the "proportion of recreative reading in a public library is necessarily large. In like manner," he said,

> the greater proportion of those who visit a zoological or botanical
> garden do so for amusement. Yet the information that they secure in so
> doing is none the less valuable and both are certainly educational
> institutions. So if in the public library a large number of its users get
> their history, their travel and their biography through the medium of
> recreative readings we should not complain. Were it otherwise
> these readers would probably lack altogether the information that they
> now certainly acquire.[20]

Similarly, other librarians proposed that the reading of current fiction could be as great a benefit as, or even greater than, the prescribed reading of nonfiction, because an idea or moral could often be conveyed more effectively in fiction than in other literary forms.

Although there was no longer any question among the majority of librarians as to the provision of current fiction, a few, however, were opposed to the practice of responding wholly to community demands, maintaining that this led to the relegation of the library to the "amusement column." Arthur H. Chamberlain, representing the National Education Association at the 1911 ALA Conference, observed that "some libraries, and the major portion of most, I fear, judged by the books on their shelves, belong with the theatre and the summer resort. A collection of books meeting this requirement *merely* is not a library."[21] Differences of opinion were not about the inclusion or exclusion of fiction, or about fiction versus nonfiction, but mainly about the quality of fiction being provided by public libraries.

Herbert Putnam stated that librarians were "conceding too much to the demand for recreative literature of inferior literary worth," and that the "old excuse for such concession (i.e., the use of such books as 'bait') no longer applies, and never applied to the class in the community whom it was most worthwhile to attract."[22] Even assuming that reading taste could be elevated by beginning at the reader's level, Putnam doubted that this could be accomplished by providing second-rate novels that were inferior in style. "We do not deliberately furnish poor art at public expense," he said, "because there is a portion of the public which cannot appreciate the better. Nor when the best is offered, with apology, does the uncultured public in fact complain that it is too 'advanced.' "[23]

With the growth of public library book collections, the supply of novels of doubtful value increased. Although the original purpose for the provision of novels by public libraries was, and to some extent still is, to provide "wholesome recreation," some librarians of this period began to associate (or justify) the supplying of popular fiction with the idea of democratic library service. In a paper entitled "Should Libraries Buy Only the Best Books or the Best Books That People Will Read," Charles A. Cutter wrote:

> When you have a perfect people you can afford to have only perfect
> books, if there are such things; perhaps there will be then. When you have
> a homogeneous public you can hope to have a stock of books exactly
> fitted to them all, and no book shall be unfitted to any one of them. But so
> long as there is a public of every diversity of mental capacity, previous
> education, habits of thought, taste, ideals, you must, if you are to give them
> satisfaction or do them any good, provide many books which will suit
> and benefit some and will do no good, perhaps in some cases may do
> harm, to others. It is inevitable. There is no escape from this
> fundamental difficulty.[24]

This line of reasoning, which originated during the first decade of this century, gradually gained wider acceptance among librarians and eventually became one of the tenets of book selection practice. Out of this belief evolved the idea that the librarian's responsibility was to maintain a middle-of-the-road course between supplying (within the limits of time, staff, and budget) the books that he believed to be of value and supplying those requested by the public. Implementing this idea led to the development of library collections consisting of books of various levels of quality. This practice, it was assumed, was not only inevitable but necessary because by providing so-called "good," "average," and even "mediocre" or "poor" books, public libraries permitted and even ensured individual readers the right and opportunity to form their own judgment of library books and to decide what they wished to read. Accepting the fact that some books were inferior in terms of literary quality, and that in some instances they exerted an undesirable

effect upon certain readers, the libraries, nevertheless, had no justification, according to this view of book selection, for depriving the majority
of readers who could safely use such books. To do so would not be in
accord with the American tradition.

H. J. de Vleeschauwer, Director of the Library School at the University of South Africa, pointed out the relationship between the democratic or liberal ideology of twentieth-century America and the recreational function of the American public library. He observed:

> However different liberalism and socialism may be in their social
> application, and though they may have become enemies in the shape of
> capitalism and Marxism, yet we should not forget that in a cultural and
> spiritual sense socialism practically grew out of the climate and ideology of
> Enlightenment. Whereas liberalism, if not in theory then at least in
> practice, brought the recreational function of the library to the fore,
> socialism consciously promoted its educational function. It is remarkable
> how sharp a division in the library field to which this development
> gave rise has prevailed since the 19th century.[25]

In summary, then, it may be said that the provision of popular fiction
by public libraries was first qualified under the term "wholesome recreation" and then associated with a theory of democratic library service,
which emphasized the indeterminate idea of the observance of the rights
of the library user. Differences of opinion about popular fiction during
this period were more often pleasantly rationalized than critically examined. But underlying these differences was a fundamental and growing
conflict about the ends that a public library should seek to attain.

Informational Reference Service

During the early 1900's, informational reference service was instituted
in many small public libraries and extended in urban libraries. As the
number of trained librarians increased, this service became more widespread, more systematically organized, and more effective. In addition
to locating information for the casual questioner, many of the reference
librarians of this period instructed the public in the use of reference
books, answered reference questions by mail and telephone, and established cooperative systems of interlibrary loan.[26]

After 1910, when reference service was generally available in branch
libraries of city systems and in most small public libraries, steps were
taken to publicize reference service and to create an image of the library as an information center. In the urban libraries, reference collections became more specialized, the assistance rendered became more
knowledgeable and thorough, and emphasis was placed on serving the
informational needs of special groups, particularly businessmen. In small
libraries, reference service was usually confined, because of limitations of
reference collections, to fact finding of a general nature.[27]

Educational Responsibility

Educational Objective

Although the extension of service to new areas and to children and the provision of recreational and informational services were uppermost in the minds of the majority of librarians, the educational objective was not altogether forgotten. Between 1900 and 1917, some librarians, pointing out that it was for educational ends that the founders of public libraries had justified their proposals, declared that the library's educational responsibility was valid because the public schools provided only a method, a mode of approach to subjects; no system of education did more than assist the individual to educate himself; and no other agency was equipped to assist persons to continue their education along informal lines.

As a result of the widespread development of elementary school education and the steady growth of the secondary school in this country between 1890 and 1920,[28] librarians, during the first two decades of this century, adjusted their educational objective to changing conditions—to provide adults, particularly those unable either to attend high school or to complete it, with the means to continue their education.[29]

Educational Role

The advocates of the library's educational responsibility considered the public library to be not just an adjunct of the public schools but an integral part of the educational system. "The school and the library," said Arthur H. Chamberlain, "are parts of one and the same great organic institution."[30] The school stood for the acquisition of knowledge and the library for the rounding out of this knowledge.[31] Although both institutions had similar ends, the methods of each were different. "The school is formal in its approach, the library is informal in the extreme. Back of the teacher is all the power of the state, back of the librarian is nothing but her own ability to persuade."[32] Several prominent library leaders of this period—Frederick M. Crunden, Librarian of the St. Louis Public Library; Ernest C. Richardson, Librarian of the Princeton University Library; and Walter L. Brown, Librarian of the Buffalo Public Library—urged librarians to help create among the general population a conception of the public library as a "people's university," a community institution whose educational role was to take up the education of citizens at the point where it was discontinued by the public schools. And the library's duty toward adult learners, stated Brown, was probably more important than its duty toward that class of individuals still in school.[33]

Educational Goals and Services

Most of the educational services provided by the public libraries of this period were directed toward two goals: personal development, with particular attention to the enrichment of human life,[34] and civic enlightenment, with special emphasis on the Americanization of non-English-speaking immigrants.[35]

Libraries in the principal cities—New York City, Brooklyn, Chicago, Detroit, and Seattle—assisted in the Americanization of the vast number of immigrants entering this country between 1900 and 1915. These libraries provided the newly arrived alien with the best literature of his own country as well as readable books about America, its institutions, customs, and ideals. Libraries also organized classes in beginning English and cosponsored citizenship instruction.[36] A vast literature about ways that libraries could help to assimilate the immigrant was developed during these years, perhaps because for the first time libraries could pursue an educational goal that not only was specific but also had immediate social implications.

In addition to providing materials and personal assistance, librarians of this period began to devise methods to stimulate adults to read material of educational value. This was done by preparing and distributing book lists, setting up book displays, and giving book talks. Some libraries also provided program assistance to community organizations, sponsored lecture series, and assisted in the planning of women's study club programs.[37] But, except for the large urban libraries that furnished special services for immigrants, the educational efforts of the majority of public libraries of this period were meager.

Some of the librarians who did the most to stimulate self-education through libraries were rather discouraged. If the library, in serving a vast and heterogeneous constituency, sought to "assume the position of an educator," stated Herbert Putnam, "it finds that its authority is one which the constituents themselves are unanimously unwilling to concede."[38] The library world as a whole, recognizing that only a minority of the population continued their education into adult life, had—asserted Edwin W. Gaillard, Librarian of the Webster Free Library of New York City—"made up its mind that the people have no use for books for serious study."[39] The vast majority of adult readers, it was concluded, had not been trained in the technique indispensable to self-education, namely, the getting of ideas and information independently from books. In 1917, Walter L. Brown, then President of the American Library Association, said that librarians "must admit that in large measure any real training by the use of books our readers may receive is, for the most part, a matter of chance."[40] The Director of the Carnegie Library of Pittsburgh, John H. Leete, summarized, in 1919, the librarian's dilemma in trying to direct more attention to the library's educational aim:

There is no occasion to speak of one function of the library. We, all of us, know its value as a recreational agency in the community. Indeed, the public too often regards this as the sole purpose of the library's existence. Too many think of it as a place where one may borrow without expense the transient novel that he does not consider worth buying for himself. Yet that statement is hardly fair to the public library, cosmopolitan and charitable as it must be to satisfy the widely varying tastes of its community. For we know that even a public library exercises some discrimination in the choice of its books, and it does try, by hook and by crook, to interest readers in things worth reading.[41]

Conflict between Educational Ideals and Practice

Librarians succeeded, between 1898 and 1919, in making libraries more accessible, in increasing library use, and in providing service to children. These were definite accomplishments. However, with so much attention on the rapid extension of services and on giving the public the kind of books it wanted, a subsequent reduction of standards was evident. The seriousness of the situation was commented on in 1918 by William W. Bishop:

> There is on us a very real conflict between quality and quantity, between loyalty to our professional ideals, what we know to be good service, and the pressure of an ever-increasing demand. Never have we seen so many things to be done, or felt so keenly our own call to serve. There is a disquieting disposition to spread our energies over too great a number of things, to take on too much work, and to advertise far beyond our ability to perform. It is a very insidious temptation and I believe it assails the heads of small libraries even more subtly than their colleagues with greater and heavier demands and resources.[42]

Without minimizing the hard work, the good intentions, and the positive accomplishments of the librarians of this period, it is evident, in retrospect, that some of these dedicated individuals were responsible for creating serious problems for the next generation of public librarians. Over and above the desire to reach more people, the missionary librarians of the early-twentieth century often broadened library services without quite knowing for what purpose these services were being extended. Concerned with increasing library use, they made many compromises with popular demand, resulting in the great preponderance of light fiction that characterizes the library collections of many small libraries today. In an effort to serve the entire community, they attempted to be all things to all men. The ultimate consequence was a general confusion of library aims.

The recreation and the informational reference objectives of public libraries were fully recognized during this period. In terms of practice, the majority of libraries placed major emphasis on recreation, with reference and education occupying second and third places, respectively:[43]

1. Recreational reading through public libraries became widespread by sheer, overwhelming quantity. The turnover of popular novels produced impressive circulation figures which were often used with public officials to obtain increases in library support. But once circulation figures were accepted as a standard for measuring library service, many librarians discovered that, in order to increase circulation each year, they had to add more and more current fiction as a means of retaining a sizable portion of library users.
2. Informational reference service, increasing in scope and importance, became a highly specialized service representing a substantial claim on the librarian's time and on the library budget.
3. Educational services were, for the most part, marginal and without direction and plan. The majority of librarians made relatively few attempts to improve or increase the educational work of libraries. But the minority who did (excluding those who were providing well-directed educational services to immigrants) were somewhat disillusioned concerning the efficacy of the library as an educational institution.

The ambiguity of library aims which arose during this period came about as librarians realized that they must state, as a theoretical assumption in all public pronouncements, that the public library was first and foremost an educational institution, which provided education, information, and recreation. But it was necessary, in terms of actual practice, that the order of emphasis be: recreation, information, and education. The only library objective with a clear-cut position, in terms of both theory and practice, was informational reference service. The general status of the public library as an educational agency would soon change, to some extent, as a result of librarians' participation in the Library War Service Program.

Library War Service Program

The Library War Service Program, established to provide library service to the soldiers and sailors of this country during World War I, was a civilian enterprise organized by the American Library Association. Fund-raising and book-donation drives were conducted in 1917 and 1918, and funds were provided by the Carnegie Corporation for the construction of library buildings at thirty-six large army posts. By the end of 1919, $6,000,000 had been expended on books and library service, and 7,000,000 volumes had been placed in Library War Service libraries or distributed directly to Army and Navy personnel.[44]

More than 700 librarians participated in the Library War Service Program for periods varying from several months to two or three years. In working with servicemen, many librarians had their first major experience in providing personal guidance to readers. This phase of library work had an energizing effect on the profession as a whole. William Warner Bishop, in his presidential address to the members of the ALA Conference in 1919, said that, as a result of the Library War Service Program, the value and need of the librarian's work in collecting and interpreting books had at last gained recognition. As librarians, he said, "we are at the crossroads; we are conscious today of greater possibilities in library work and in the concerted work of librarians than we ever sensed in days gone by."[45]

In 1920, some librarians, particularly those who had taken part in the Library War Service Program and had subsequently begun to distrust a purely quantitative assessment of library service, turned their attention to serving the individual reader.

Chapter

IV

Serving the Individual
1920–1940

In the interval between the end of World War I and the beginning of World War II, the number of public libraries providing adult educational services increased, and the way in which these services were provided helped to attract an increasing number of adults. These advances came about because more librarians were confirmed in the belief that they were capable of employing their resources and their energies in direct educational processes.

American Library Association Leadership

The work of the American Library Association in adult education during the 1920's and 1930's was carried out by the ALA Commission on the Library and Adult Education (1924–1926), the ALA Board on the Library and Adult Education (1926–1937), and the ALA Adult Education Board (1937–1940).

Background, 1920–1924

The appointment of the ALA Commission on the Library and Adult Education marked the beginning of organized library adult education in this country. The events that led to the establishment of the Commission and subsequently influenced the direction of its work were the initiation of the ALA Enlarged Program, the organization of readers' services in five urban libraries, and the publication of William S. Learned's *The American Public Library and the Diffusion of Knowledge.*[1]

The Library War Service Program (1917–1919) had several consequences for the public librarian of 1920. First, the American men who had been exposed to this program during the war constituted a new audience of potential readers. Second, librarians had been successful in guiding the reading of servicemen during the war. In 1920, attempts were made to find a means of utilizing this experience and applying the lessons of the military camp to the civilian population. Out of a desire on the part of librarians to find a way to utilize their personal skills more fully in assisting readers came the conviction that the educational commitment of the public library was still a valid one and needed to be revitalized. Many librarians, especially the younger, professionally trained librarians and those who had assisted with the War Service Program, were not content to perpetuate prewar policies and methods. "We, as librarians," proclaimed the ALA Executive Board, "could never again be satisfied with pre-war library conditions. We have seen bigger things. With our responsibility to the War and Navy Departments discharged, what then lies before us?"[2] The answer was the ALA Enlarged Program, which was adopted by the ALA Executive Board in 1920.

This program consisted of six proposed activities: (1) adult self-education through the provision of lists and reading courses, (2) institutional library work, (3) service to the foreign-born, (4) books for the blind, (5) library extension, and (6) a survey of libraries.[3] After four months of intensive effort to raise funds, the organizing committee concluded that the attempt to finance the program was unsuccessful, and it was officially terminated in October, 1920.[4] Although the program did not materialize, the hope and enthusiasm with which it was launched did not subside. Two important developments resulted: some librarians gave increased attention to the provision of educational services for adults, and the Carnegie Corporation became interested in the program, notably the adult education aspects, and later made it possible for the American Library Association to undertake some of the proposed activities.

In the early 1920's, some of the leaders in the library profession had a fairly clear perception of their opportunity in the field of adult education.[5] Between 1922 and 1924, five urban public libraries began to experiment in providing assistance to adults in search of informal education through reading. Separate departments for this service were established in the public libraries of Detroit and Cleveland in 1922, of Chicago and Milwaukee in 1923, and of Indianapolis in 1924.[6]

The provision of readers' advisory service was an attempt to assist the adult whose need for books and guidance could not be met by the busy librarian at the circulation desk or by the reference librarian. This type of service was clearly distinguished from the assistance provided by a reference department. The function of the readers' adviser was to plan personalized reading programs and to select materials in accordance with the individual's reading ability, while the work of the reference librarian was to supply information and sources of information. The ideal of readers' advisory service was to give informed and sympathetic advice to the individual on his reading needs, with the adviser serving as the link between the books and the reader.

During the period from 1921 to 1923, William S. Learned, a member of the staff of the Carnegie Foundation for the Advancement of Teaching, studied public library problems and prepared a memorandum describing the results of his study. The trustees of the Carnegie Corporation of New York thought that Learned's presentation was so informative and discerning that it deserved to be published. In June, 1924, Learned's report, *The American Public Library and the Diffusion of Knowledge,* was published in book form. It was the first detailed and systematic plan for making the public library predominantly an educational institution.

Learned envisioned the public library as a medium for circulating ideas. By utilizing the available cultural and informational resources, such as lantern slides, recordings, exhibits, lectures, forums, and artworks, the public library could become, according to Learned, a "community intelligence center."[7] Instead of the library's being a place merely for the storage of certain traditional bodies of knowledge contained in books, said Learned, it could become "the warehouse and market exchange for all permanently important or temporarily useful information, in whatever form, that a given community may find to its advantage."[8] He challenged librarians to make the public library an institution for the effective diffusion of knowledge and thereby to increase the opportunities for adults to learn. Although his proposal was praised by some librarians, others contended that his vision of the public library of the future was rather grandiose and somewhat unrealistic for an institution primarily concerned with the collection and utilization of books.

Three major developments, then, were instrumental in the establishment of the ALA Commission on the Library and Adult Education and subsequently influenced the direction of its work: (1) the interest in reader guidance that grew out of the Library War Service Program and later became a major area of concern in the proposed ALA Enlarged Program; (2) the experimental work of five urban libraries in providing reader guidance; and (3) the interest of the Carnegie Corporation in the educational aspects of the ALA Enlarged Program and the educational potential of public libraries as described by Learned.[9]

ALA Commission on the Library and Adult Education

In June, 1924, Frederick P. Keppel, President of the Carnegie Corporation of New York, called a meeting of the representatives of various educational agencies to discuss whether there were sufficient common

interests and activities to warrant the establishment of a national adult
education association. On the basis of the deliberations of this group,
it was decided that the first step would be to determine the character and
scope of nonvocational adult education in the United States. To accomplish this purpose, the Carnegie Corporation provided the funds for
undertaking five studies, four of which were made by investigators working in cooperation with the staff of the Carnegie Corporation. The fifth
was conducted by the ALA Commission on the Library and Adult Education.[10]

The members of the Commission on the Library and Adult Education,
appointed in July, 1924, by the ALA Executive Board, were authorized
"to study and investigate the role of the library in adult education."[11]
The work of the Commission, supported by an initial grant of $24,500
from the Carnegie Corporation, was carried out by six chief librarians[12]
under the direction of Judson T. Jennings, Librarian of the Seattle
Public Library and then President of the American Library Association.
In his presidential address, Jennings discussed the educational function
of the public library and described the lines along which the work of the
Commission would be conducted.[13] In contrast with William Learned's
conception of the public library as a "community intelligence center,"
Jennings maintained that it was not the proper function of a library to
serve as an art gallery, museum, or community center; to provide lantern
slides and phonograph records; to conduct lecture series; or to organize
formal classes. The legitimacy of any library service, he asserted, depended upon its relation to the promotion of reading. Thus, the work
of the Commission, he said, would be directed toward studying the
informal services of libraries and then recommending, on the basis of
the findings of the study, the most appropriate ways in which libraries
could take their place in the adult educational movement.

The Commission, which was in existence from July, 1924, to October,
1926, accomplished much in a short time. The members of the Commission began the publication of *Adult Education and the Library,* a
bulletin containing information concerning library practice in adult
education; appointed a Subcommittee on Readable Books to investigate
procedures for encouraging the production of books of educational
value; developed, in cooperation with the ALA Editorial Committee,
the "Reading with a Purpose" publication program, a series of courses
designed to promote self-education through systematic reading and
study; conducted a two-year study of the library's role in adult education
and described the findings of this study in a report, *Libraries and Adult
Education;* and recommended the establishment of a permanent Board
on the Library and Adult Education to continue the work of the temporary Commission.

In November, 1925, the Commission issued the first in the series of bulletins called *Adult Education and the Library*. The aims of this publication were to report what libraries were doing in adult education; encourage librarians to evaluate the work of their libraries; stimulate the study of adult education as a necessary foundation for an understanding of the place of the public library in American life and of its relation to other agencies of adult education; promote cooperation between libraries and these other agencies; and keep librarians and the public informed of the progress and findings of the Commission.[14]

Although the primary emphasis of this publication was on the provision of readers' advisory service, articles describing other activities were included, such as those on organizing discussion groups; providing educational services to industrial workers, older boys and girls out of school, businessmen, and residents of rural areas; and establishing cooperative relations between libraries and university extension divisions. Among the contributors to the bulletin were many of the outstanding adult educators of this period: Morse A. Cartwright, John Chancellor, Jennie M. Flexner, Judson T. Jennings, Frederick P. Keppel, and Everett Dean Martin.

As a corollary to the emphasis on readers' advisory service, readable books became a focus of attention. In providing service to adults who wished to continue their education through reading, librarians found that the majority of adult books were addressed to readers of superior education and background and that most informative books were too long and too difficult for the reader with limited education. It was estimated that 30 percent of the persons wishing to pursue a reading course needed specially written books.[15] In recognition of this need, a Subcommittee on Readable Books was appointed by the Commission in July, 1925.

In its first report the Subcommittee defined the various grades of readability, presented a list of selected titles to illustrate the type of books that should be published, identified areas in which readable books were needed, and conferred with publishers about ways to stimulate the production of readable books. During the next ten years, the members of the Subcommittee conducted studies and compiled lists of the most readable and available books. The first study published was Emma Felsenthal's *Readable Books in Many Subjects*,[16] which included a description of the qualities of readability and a list of available books meeting these criteria. Other work of the Subcommittee included cooperation in the reading studies of William S. Gray of the University of Chicago and of Edward L. Thorndike of Teachers College, Columbia University.

In an effort to extend readers' advisory service, the American Library Association published, in May, 1925, the first pamphlet in a series called "Reading with a Purpose." This series of reading courses, initiated by the members of the Commission in cooperation with the ALA Editorial Committee and made possible by a special grant from the Carnegie Corporation, was prepared by the executive assistant to the Commission and his associates. Between 1925 and 1933, sixty-seven of these courses were issued. They covered a wide variety of subjects, such as biology, English literature, economics, journalism, music appreciation, and philosophy. Each was prepared by a widely known subject specialist whose aim was "to make the course popular and at the same time fundamentally sound."[17] Each course consisted of an introductory essay—which suggested to the reader the interest, pleasure, and profit to be found in the subject—followed by descriptions of eight to twelve books listed in the order in which they should be read for further knowledge of the subject.

The "Reading with a Purpose" series was one of the most widely publicized and discussed projects of this period. In 1929, Frederick P. Keppel stated that most of the ALA reading courses were excellent but that, in his opinion, few individuals would complete a reading program alone. He urged librarians to make opportunities available for individuals pursuing the same reading course to come together for discussion.[18] A different type of criticism of the series was made by Edward F. Stevens, Director of the School of Library Science at Pratt Institute, who questioned both the value of the project and the assumption upon which it was undertaken:

> The *Reading with a Purpose* program is a commendable effort on the part of Headquarters with abundance of means, and seeking outlets for expenditure. It seems a new Literary Guild to absolve librarians of independent book-choosing. They are the lists of experts, and suffer the weakness incident to knowledge of a subject without knowledge of the needs of those who are invited to approach the subject. The preparation of these lists for libraries by those who are not themselves librarians has been a severe blow to our professional pride, and the implied lack of confidence on the part of our own organization in its membership to do the work which is theirs to do, will take years to live down. They who employ librarians have taken us at our own valuation.
>
> To enlarge the library's usefulness, to enable those desirous of pursuing education after schooling to go on with learning, to direct and guide seekers after knowledge, to give opportunity to read and study to the bookless—all this and much more is elemental librarianship. That many who have entered upon the life school of experience crave culture, erudition and continuous progressive study and improvement has not been evidenced in my own observation in a quarter century's close touch with the public—not enough surely to warrant a recasting of our work in terms of the few.[19]

The total number of copies of the "Reading with a Purpose" pamphlets that were sold between 1925 and 1931 was 850,000. Nevertheless, the series was discontinued in 1933 because the courses could not be revised easily and, since they had been prepared for mass use, could not always be used effectively with adults having different reading abilities. In commenting on the overall influence of this project, John Chancellor, the ALA Specialist in Adult Education, said that the pamphlets

> have served admirably to carry the ideas, novel to many, of planned purposeful reading and of the library as an agency of informal education. Such tangible symbols are of no small value in planting new conceptions in the public mind. The series has been honored by quantities of grateful praise from the learned, from practical men, from untutored laymen, from educators and the press.[20]

In 1926, after two years of study, the ALA Commission on the Library and Adult Education submitted its report, *Libraries and Adult Education*,[21] which was an analysis of adult education possibilities for public libraries. The members of the Commission maintained that each public library had an inherent duty to assume an active role in adult education and recommended that the most appropriate ways to carry out this responsibility were:

Readers' guidance—the provision of readers' advisory service to those who wished to pursue their studies alone, rather than in organized groups or classes

Informational service—the provision of information on local opportunities for adult education outside the library

Auxiliary service—the provision of books and other printed material to other agencies engaged in adult education

The members of the Commission, in formulating their recommendations, also took into account the major obstacles that prevented libraries from effectively providing educational services and suggested means for overcoming these obstacles. The problems and suggested solutions were:

Weaknesses in the educational system. Boys and girls leaving school look upon books merely as classroom tools and not as friendly guides in the solution of life's problems or as sources of pleasure and culture. Attention, therefore, must be given to closer cooperation between librarians and educators in order that ways can be found to develop among boys and girls, before they leave school, a love of books and a permanent interest in reading and study.

Lack of qualified readers' advisers. The recognition of readers' advisory service as an important and integral activity of libraries cannot be achieved until there are more well-educated and trained advisers to work with persons who wish to continue their education through reading. Thus, library schools and the ALA Board of Education for Librarianship should be requested to consider the advisability of establishing special courses of instruction in adult education for librarians and of incorporating the necessary instruction in courses already established; and, further, the ALA should consider the advisability of conducting institutes for readers' advisers and other librarians engaged in special adult education service.

Lack of readable books. The lack of suitable books for mature individuals limits the effectiveness of the adult education services of libraries. Consequently, further efforts must be made to establish closer cooperation between educators, authors, and publishers for the purpose of publishing more books that are clearly and simply written and are appropriate for adult reading and study.

Inadequate supply of books. More than half of the population is without library service. Studies, therefore, must be made to find ways of supplying books to serious students who do not have access to libraries. Immediate efforts must be made to coordinate library agencies and to establish collections that are adequate and readily accessible.

The Commission, in submitting the report, stated that it claimed no great discovery: "Most of the ideas advanced are already at work somewhere in the library world. What is new is the attempt to assemble and describe these disconnected services, and to coordinate them into a definite, workable plan or program."[22] Nevertheless, the Commission's report was a thorough analysis of fundamental problems and the first comprehensive statement of a program of adult education through libraries, with particular emphasis on philosophy, objectives, and methods. This report not only reflected the character of most adult education activity among libraries of the time but also established a precedent for the nature of such work for the next fifteen years.

The report also recommended that the Council of the American Library Association appoint a permanent Board on the Library and Adult Education and maintain a staff at the ALA Headquarters to carry out activities designed to assist libraries to develop adult education services. The Commission offered the following suggestions toward a program for the permanent Board:

Continue the publication, *Adult Education and the Library*

Prepare a manual on library service in adult education

Publish additional courses in the "Reading with a Purpose" series

Initiate library experiments and demonstrations in adult education

Study the development of reading habits

Establish cooperative relations with national organizations whose programs include phases of adult education

Inaugurate a program of education that will arouse librarians, library trustees, educational authorities, and appropriating bodies to the possibilities of the library as an adult education agency

The recommendations were concluded with this statement:

The value of the work of the present Commission and the permanent
Board will depend not alone upon the practicability of their
recommendations, but also upon the extent to which libraries can be
persuaded to adopt them. If librarians will undertake serious work in adult
education and if they can demonstrate to the general public the feasibility
of the idea of education through reading, this new "university"
will not lack for "students."[23]

The response of the library profession to the work of the Commission
was directed toward such problems as the interpretation of adult education services of libraries, the use of appropriate methods in providing
these services, the effect of adult education on libraries, and the necessity
of obtaining public acceptance of the educational work of libraries. In
1925, William E. Henry, Director of the School of Library Science at
the University of Washington, predicted that adult education was perhaps the most significant opportunity that had come to the library profession, but he warned librarians not to interpret every device they em-
ployed as "a great advance and call it adult education." Librarians,
Henry continued, may suddenly find that some of their work *is* adult
education and may be as surprised as was Mr. Jourdain when he discovered, in "The Shopkeeper Turned Gentleman," that he had been
speaking prose for forty years without being aware of it.[24]

The majority of pronouncements about the work of the Commission
were not about the why or what of the library and adult education but
mainly about how the library should perform this function. In contrast
with the conservative suggestions of the Commission, the noted educator
Eduard C. Lindeman asserted that if libraries were to become creative
centers of learning, "experimentation must be initiated."[25] Four months
after Lindeman's statement was published, Herman H. B. Meyer, then
President of the American Library Association, pointed out that although
adult education was perhaps the most important phase of the library's
work, librarians should carry out this function by proceeding on "essen-
tially library lines and not on school lines."[26]

The next ALA president, Charles F. D. Belden, expressed the hope
that in the future the library would become a greater agency of adult
education, and suggested that this could be accomplished through increased publicity and work with the foreign-born, the unassimilated
alien, the blind, and the hospital patient. He concluded his presidential
address by predicting that the work of the Commission and its relation
to the work of the adult educational movement would prove to be the
beginning of revitalized service in many small libraries across the nation
—a rejustification for their existence.[27] At this same meeting, Melvil
Dewey praised the efforts of those who were reconstructing the public
library along educational lines and recommended that the next impor-

tant step be "to win complete public acceptance of the theory we have been preaching for years. . . . It can be done only by making people wish for the best thing, and that process is education."[28]

ALA Board on the Library and Adult Education

On October 4, 1926, the Commission on the Library and Adult Education was dissolved, and the ALA Council voted to create a permanent Board on the Library and Adult Education to succeed the temporary Commission. The Board, composed of five members, was assigned the tasks of continuing the studies inaugurated by the Commission and of providing information and advice to librarians interested in developing educational services.[29] In their first report, the members of the Board stated that present conditions called for a new emphasis, that while "investigations and study must continue to a certain extent, the period of intensive study has ended. The next step will be to get into *practice* the basic ideas set forth in *Libraries and Adult Education*."[30]

The need for implementation was emphasized further by George H. Locke, President of the American Library Association in 1927. In his presidential address, Locke suggested that librarians had so frequently been told that the public library was an educational institution that the idea was in danger of becoming a platitude. "I can imagine," he said, "no worse fate than that we should tolerate platitudes, those fervent statements on the platform which deal in generalities and which not only do not land us anywhere but drug men's minds till they cannot see what action is really called for, and still less to rise to any action." The educational commitment, continued Locke, was the librarian's major responsibility. And do not forget, he said, that "education is a process that is ever going on. Were it not so there would be much less excuse for the presence of such an institution as the library."[31]

During the latter half of the 1920's, it was stated frequently in the pages of *Adult Education and the Library* and by presidents of the American Library Association that educational service to adults was the library's primary responsibility and, therefore, the public library should become one of the principal agencies in the adult educational movement. However, the extent to which it could or should assume this role was questioned. Carl Roden, Librarian of the Chicago Public Library, suggested in 1928[32] that the ALA Board on the Library and Adult Education was appropriately named. It is, he said, "the Board on the Library *and* Adult Education, not on the Library *in* or *for*." He proposed that these two concepts were "separate and coordinate," pointing out that the public library could be of value to any educational agency and especially to the informal type. But our chief concern at present, he said, "is still how far the library may penetrate into any part of the educational field and retain the precious freedom it prizes so highly."[33]

In January, 1931, Francis K. W. Drury, the Executive Assistant to the Board, reported on the work of the Association in adult education from 1924 to 1930. "The outstanding accomplishments during the past six years," wrote Drury, "would seem to be four: cooperation with national organizations, the Reading with a Purpose Courses, Emma Felsenthal's *Readable Books in Many Subjects,* and the encouragement of readers' advisory service."[34] As to the future activities of the Board, Drury pointed out that primary emphasis would be placed on the extension of existing projects "rather than on any new or startling developments."[35]

With the impact of the Depression[36] and with the gradual expiration of Carnegie Funds, the income of the Board was reduced, and most of its activities were curtailed. For a period of three years, the Board was without an Executive Assistant. Then, in 1934, significant leadership in library adult education was once again resumed by the Association when John Chancellor joined the ALA Headquarters staff as assistant in adult education.

In 1935, Chancellor reviewed the work of the American Library Association in adult education from 1924 to 1934 and commented on the overall accomplishments: librarians had become aware of adult education as a main objective; the adult education services of libraries had increased, particularly the provision of readers' advisory service; and librarians had been successful in introducing the idea of informal education through reading to millions of adults. Two of the most significant changes, wrote Chancellor, were that "the associated adult educationists are prone to think and refer to the library as one of the fundamental stones in the adult education structure. And as for the general public that patronizes libraries, it is a conservative guess that ten now think of the library as a place for informal education to one who so thought of it in 1924."[37]

ALA Adult Education Board

In 1937, the Board on the Library and Adult Education was renamed the Adult Education Board. Prior to this time, the direction of the Association's work in adult education had been in the hands of chief librarians. However, from 1937 to 1955, the Board was composed primarily of staff librarians, most of whom were engaged exclusively in the provision of educational services to adults. Reflecting the interests of its members, the new Board first made four suggestions on ways in which the public library could become a more vital force in the adult education movement: (1) promote publication of readable books; (2) eliminate library routine that interfered with the effective performance of the adult educational function; (3) make more use of audio-visual materials; and (4) consider the possibilities of forming discussion groups and sponsoring lecture courses.[38] The following year, the Board commented on the growth of various types of educational services through libraries and concluded that "service to the individual in search of self-education" was what the Board considered to be the "library's primary adult education function."[39]

In 1939, the members of the Board began to prepare descriptions of service schemes in adult education from which libraries could pick one or more plans that seemed suited to trial in local situations. These plans were to be experiments in "mental reorganization."[40] This work,[41] which was completed in 1940, represented the advanced thinking of the time. It suggested a wide range of educational activities for libraries, such as remedial reading clinics, a new subject classification based on readers' interests, the preparation of annotated cards in the library catalog, reader guidance through the newspaper, a vocational guidance service, and a library psychologist.

Thus, the work of the American Library Association in adult education from 1924 to 1940 consisted of securing foundation funds for experimentation, initiating projects to increase the educational effectiveness of libraries, and encouraging librarians to put more emphasis on serving the educational needs of the individual reader. The additive effect of the leadership provided by the Association can be shown by examining the growth, direction, and methodology of the adult educational services provided by public libraries during this period.

Educational Services for Adults

The adult educational services provided by public libraries between 1920 and 1940 were directed toward three main goals: personal development, vocational improvement, and civic enlightenment. Between 1920 and 1929 the major educational emphasis was on personal development: helping individuals extend their cultural background, satisfying social and spiritual needs, and furthering avocational interests.[42] Then, with the coming of the Depression, librarians turned their attention to vocational improvement. From 1930 to 1935, they helped individuals to increase their vocational competence, to acquire new skills, and to prepare themselves for their role in the post-Depression society.[43] By 1936, other problems emerged that were as disturbing as those produced by the Depression. The rapid spread of totalitarianism became a serious danger to the free nations. From 1936 to 1938, librarians encouraged individuals to increase their understanding of the ideologies that threatened the American form of government and to develop critical attitudes toward what they heard and read.[44] Then in 1939, when the peace of the world was shattered by the outbreak of war, the educational goal of public libraries shifted to helping individuals increase their understanding of democratic traditions.[45]

The major types of adult educational services provided by public libraries during this period were readers' advisory service, auxiliary service to other organizations engaged in adult education, and sponsorship of discussion groups.

Readers' Advisory Service

Readers' advisory service represented a significant advance in librarianship. In contrast to the earlier routine lending of books and supplying of information, reader guidance was a personalized service that helped to create a clearer image of the librarian as an educator.

The readers' adviser was a specially qualified person on the library staff free to give unhurried consultation and aid to individuals desiring to read to some specific end, and to plan special courses of reading suited to each individual's needs and abilities. The two central objectives of the readers' adviser were to assist adults in achieving their own learning goals and to help change random readers into purposeful readers. Reader guidance passed through three phases of development between 1922 and 1940. The first occurred in the years between 1922 and 1926; the second, from 1927 to 1935; the third, from 1936 to 1940.

Between 1922 and 1925, readers' advisory services were instituted in seven urban public libraries: Detroit and Cleveland (1922); Chicago and Milwaukee (1923); Indianapolis (1924); Cincinnati and Portland, Oregon (1925).[46] During this period, when readers' advisory work was in an experimental stage of development, the emphasis was on the provision of an "extra" service and on the "separateness" of this type of library work. Provided at first by a special librarian, reader guidance was considered to be a function apart from the other services of the library. The first group of advisers confined their work primarily to the preparation of individualized reading courses for persons who wished to read systematically to meet the practical needs of daily living, such as pursuing personal development, extending their cultural background, meeting personal-social needs, satisfying religious and spiritual needs, or furthering avocational interests.

The way in which reader guidance was provided during this period is characterized in this description of the organization of the Readers' Advisory Department of the Detroit Public Library in 1922:

> At that time it meant a desk in the open-shelf room of the circulation department and a specially designated assistant to handle requests and to bring to users of the room a consciousness of a special service. A few years later it became necessary to establish the readers' adviser in a small separate room, admirably placed between the large delivery hall and the open-shelf room. This provided more adaptable arrangements for consultation and space for a separate book collection. This collection included all titles recommended in the Reading with a Purpose

series, and any other books which had proved especially useful with
one group or another. In addition, there were the books which were
useful as tools because of bibliographies or which had particular
informational value for the readers' adviser.[47]

The second phase of development occurred during the period from
1927 to 1935, when the knowledge made available by various reading
studies provided readers' advisers with significant insights into the nature
and problems of adult reading, and subsequently helped to improve the
effectiveness and to increase the scope of readers' advisory service.

In 1928, readers' advisory service was being provided by twenty-five
libraries; in 1930, the number increased to thirty; and by 1935, there
were sixty-three advisers in forty-four public libraries of varying sizes
and types. Hazel Webster Byrnes, Librarian of Teachers College, Columbia University, commenting on the rapid increase of this service,
suggested that it "shows evidence of becoming, as it were, the tail which
may wag the dog."[48] The main reasons for the growth of this service
were: (1) the increased number of professional workers in public libraries; (2) the increased idleness and leisure caused by the Depression,
a period in which a considerable number of adults began to read and
study to increase their vocational competence and to prepare for new
types of positions; and (3) the beginning of systematic research relating
to the problems of adult reading.

During the late 1920's and early 1930's, several aspects of reading
were studied by members of the faculty of the University of Chicago in
cooperation with the ALA Committee To Study the Development of
Reading Habits. William S. Gray and Ruth Munroe, in 1928, undertook
to discover the factors that caused some persons to acquire desirable
habits of reading. In their *Reading Interests and Habits of Adults,*[49]
they described the major purposes of readers; stated that such factors as
educational level, age, and marital status influenced the reading habits
of individuals; and concluded that reading was difficult for the average
person because he had the reading ability of only a sixth-grader.

Douglas Waples and Ralph W. Tyler presented their findings relating
to the reading interests of adults in 1931 in *What People Want To Read
About.*[50] They found that the elements that differentiated reading interests were sex, education, occupation, and geographical environment, with
the greatest difference in reading interest correlating with sex. The one
factor on which there was the most agreement was that people liked to
read about subjects that were familiar and related to themselves. The
authors concluded their study by indicating the difficulty of identifying
specific trends and making generalizations about patterns of reading
interests.

In the studies that followed the Waples and Tyler research, it was
shown that stated interest was not so important a factor in determining

what a person would read as the accessibility of reading materials, since the books a person would like to read were not always available, and the subjects he was interested in were not always "readable" in respect to vocabulary, style, and treatment.[51] In 1935, William S. Gray and Bernice E. Leary, in their work, *What Makes a Book Readable*,[52] described the various elements in writing that made for ease or difficulty in reading. The study contributed much to the early work of the Readability Laboratory, which was established in 1935 at Teachers College, Columbia University, under the direction of Lyman L. Bryson, an outstanding adult educator. The Laboratory, organized through the efforts of the ALA Subcommittee on Readable Books and the Joint ALA-American Association for Adult Education Committee on Reading Habits, was founded as an advisory bureau on readability to experiment in writing, editing, and analyzing readable material. This work resulted in the preparation of a series of volumes issued under the title of *The People's Library*.[53]

The various studies of reading and readability conducted during this period helped to provide a reliable basis for the formulation of methods for adapting book selection to the reading interests, habits, and abilities of adults and, in general, increased the effectiveness of readers' advisory service.

The third phase in the development of readers' advisory service occurred during the period from 1936 to 1940, when several patterns for providing this service emerged. In some medium-sized libraries with a full-time readers' adviser, the responsibility for assisting readers was spread throughout the library staff so as to increase the coverage of this service. In some large libraries, which may be broadly defined as those serving a population of more than 300,000 persons, the readers' bureau gradually became a referral office where requests for individual assistance were directed to the various subject departments of the library.

There were specific advantages to having a subject specialist as an adviser: the subject specialist in charge of a department brought to the position comprehensive knowledge of a particular subject; the reader benefited from having all the materials in which he was interested brought together and having a subject specialist available for consultation who knew the collection. Moreover, the subject specialist was able to evaluate books in terms of the competence of each author, to identify an author's bias, and to assess the suitability of books on a specific subject in accordance with the needs of particular readers. This approach, however, was not successful in all large libraries that shifted to this plan. The subject department plan of readers' guidance was put into effect in the Detroit Public Library, but in practice it did not work so well as expected, and a general readers' adviser section was again made available for consultation by patrons.[54]

The high point of readers' advisory service was reached during the period from 1936 to 1939, when thirty-four articles describing various aspects of this service appeared in professional library journals. However, the emphasis on readers' guidance began to shift in 1940. The outbreak of the war, with its attendant reduction in leisure time, was a major factor in diminishing the number of requests for readers' guidance. This caused some libraries either to abandon readers' guidance or to replace it with other adult services. After 1940, the number of articles in professional journals on readers' advisory service decreased markedly; during the next several years, only one or two articles a year were published.

Throughout the 1920's and early 1930's, readers' advisory service was considered the public library's primary opportunity in adult education—the central means of fostering the educational use of books. This service had an appeal to librarians on two counts. First, it was a unique service that other distributors of books could not provide. Second, it was in keeping with the general character of library service in that librarians, with a minimum of intrusion, could aid individuals to achieve their learning goals.

Much of what was accomplished through the provision of readers' advisory service during this period came about through the efforts of a relatively small number of public librarians. After eighteen years of work in this area, this small group of librarians had produced a sizable body of literature relating to the psychology, techniques, and organization of readers' advisory service, and had made other members of the library profession aware that the needs of readers—as individuals and as groups with special interests—must be studied.

But during the 1930's, readers' advisory service was seriously questioned by library administrators on two counts. First, it reached a relatively small number of people and was therefore a costly service. Second, the effective provision of this service required librarians with a wide range of skills and abilities, and because there were few opportunities for acquiring the needed training, there were wide variations in the extent and quality of the service provided. Harrison W. Craver, who was serving as president of the American Library Association in 1938, pointed out that a library aspiring to be the university of the people must have more faculty than one readers' adviser. He added: "If we undertake to be the institution through which education is to be offered freely to everyone, we must obtain a clear concept of what education is and of what we must supply to our students."[55] In a similar vein, Clarence E. Sherman, Librarian of the Providence (Rhode Island) Public Library, speaking at the 1938 Library Institute at the University of Chicago, reminded librarians that

. . . the long-cherished hope that the free public library would press on from the environment of its earlier years to reach a constantly expanding population, book-conscious and reading-desirous, until every person who has acquired the mechanics of how to read almost automatically becomes a frequenter of public libraries—this rosy-hued prospect librarians at last realized must be discarded. Too many people find reading a painful experience. Even books with reliable text, appropriate vocabulary, and good looks are no guarantee of success.[56]

Auxiliary Services to Other Organizations

Although the primary educational emphasis of this period was on readers' advisory service, public libraries also provided information concerning local opportunities for adult education and library services to other organizations engaged in adult education. This latter service included preparing program materials and reading lists for discussion or study groups; supplying books and other library materials for community organizations and for university extension and correspondence students; providing library facilities for lectures and forums; encouraging the use of library meeting rooms by community study groups, university extension classes, and discussion groups; and assisting in the establishment of local adult education councils.

Between 1933 and 1938, public libraries cooperated with various federal agencies that were organizing educational programs for adults. The American Library Association, state library commissions, and local libraries assisted in supplying books for the educational and vocational programs of the Civilian Conservation Corps. Individual libraries provided collections of books for use by students of the Emergency Education Program. And, beginning in 1936, libraries assisted with the Public Forum Program of the U.S. Office of Education by preparing exhibits and providing follow-up reading materials at the forum meetings.[57] All the above services were within the scope of the recommendations made by the ALA Commission in 1926 and generally accepted by the library profession as being appropriate for a public library to provide.

Sponsorship of Discussion Groups

During the latter part of the 1920's, some librarians began to think about the development of a more active and independent program of adult education through libraries. After gaining experience in helping to plan programs, prepare reading lists, select materials, and provide facilities for use by study and discussion groups, these librarians believed that the organization of the library's own discussion program was a natural next step. For them, the library-sponsored discussion group was another means of using the librarian's skills and the library's resources. Many other librarians, however, thought this type of service was not in accord with the traditional concept of librarianship but was merely a fad that represented the younger librarians' desire for innovation.

The decision of librarians to organize discussion groups came about through a slow, evolutionary process. The members of the ALA Commission on the Library and Adult Education, in their 1926 report, *Libraries and Adult Education,* devoted one page to discussion groups and suggested:

> Librarians may hesitate before entering on a venture which involves
> the organization and supervision of study or discussion groups.
> It is possible, however, that they may serve as the coordinating agency
> between readers and discussion leaders. This may be done in one
> of the following ways: by putting readers in touch with discussion groups
> already organized; by arranging for informal conferences between a
> public-spirited specialist and a few persons following the same reading
> course; by an arrangement with other adult education agencies whereby
> they will furnish leaders for discussion and organize small groups
> of readers. These methods have not yet been developed but they seem
> to hold considerable promise and are worthy of trial.[58]

The following year an attempt to provide a community-wide discussion program was undertaken by the Library Association of Portland, Oregon. Twenty-six groups, known as the Read-a-Book-Together clubs, were organized.[59] In 1933, several state library agencies promoted the organization of study-discussion programs on world economic conditions. And, throughout the late 1920's and early 1930's, there were a few public libraries experimenting with the sponsorship of discussion programs in Cleveland, Long Beach (California), New Haven, Cincinnati, and Detroit.[60]

By 1935, the sponsorship of discussion group programs by public libraries, although the programs were still considered to be a controversial service, was beginning to be more widespread and somewhat more acceptable. This change was in evidence, in 1935, at a three-day ALA institute on discussion methods (conducted by Lyman L. Bryson) which preceded the ALA Conference in Denver.[61] The most extensive change, however, came about in 1936 and 1937 as a result of library cooperation with the Public Forum Program of the U.S. Office of Education. In addition to supplying reading lists and materials for use at forum meetings, libraries began to organize small follow-up discussion groups for adults who attended the forum meetings.[62]

During the late 1930's, when the emphasis on reader guidance was beginning to decline, it was suggested that work with groups might be more beneficial, from an educational point of view, than readers' advisory service. Alvin Johnson, the noted social scientist, in his study, *The Public Library—A People's University,* said that "it is the rare individual who can carry his adult educational course through solitary reading." Perhaps he will "provide himself," continued Johnson,

> . . . with the finest list of books on a subject he knows to be important and may start on it with the most deliberate resolution. He will probably fall by the wayside. Personal contacts, the clash of mind upon mind, are necessary, in the great majority of cases, for persistent adult educational reading. Therefore even the best library, with the finest collection of books, cannot be a really successful adult educational institution if it confines its activities to pure librarianship.
>
> . . . .
>
> By and large, men and women require the stimulus of group activity if they are to enter seriously upon educational activity. They can not be dragooned into education, but they can be led. This function of leadership needs to be undertaken by the public library, as the one permanent organ of adult education in most communities.[63]

Another supporter of work with groups was Carleton B. Joeckel, Professor of Library Science at the University of Chicago, who suggested that this type of service helped to spread the values of reader guidance: ". . . is there any way in which the values inherent in individual guidance may be spread over a wider area without increasing the cost to prohibitive figures? The best prospect of such an achievement seems to lie in work with groups. . . ."[64]

Between 1920 and 1940, then, public librarians had become more aware of the political, social, and economic problems of the time and more confident of their ability to provide educational services to help adults understand these problems. The economic crisis of 1929 and subsequent years made librarians more socially conscious and more willing to assume new responsibilities. However, it also led to the creation of a rather awkward situation for them. While the demand for adult services increased, library funds decreased. Out of this situation developed a searching reappraisal of "essential" library services, followed by the formulation of the first ALA statement of public library objectives.

Public Library Objectives

"The best books, for the largest number, at the least cost," a slogan coined by Melvil Dewey at the ALA Conference in 1876, had, by 1910, been changed to "The right book for the individual reader at any cost." But when libraries were faced with the problem of smaller appropriations[65] and larger demands for service, the first official statement by the American Library Association on public library objectives was formulated—in 1933—with particular emphasis on defining the limits of library service:

> The public library is maintained by a democratic society in order that every man, woman, and child may have the means of self-education and

recreational reading. The library provides materials for education and advice in their use. It diffuses information and ideas necessary to the present welfare and future advancement of a community. It strengthens and extends appreciation of the cultural and spiritual values of life. It offers opportunities for constructive use of the new leisure. It serves all ages and classes.[66]

Although this statement was considered a desirable first step in clarifying the aims of public libraries, a number of prominent librarians thought that it was too broad and vague and, therefore, would not provide a clear and reliable sense of direction.

During the middle 1930's, librarians again expressed the need for a clear sense of purpose. It was suggested that, because of the lack of clearly defined objectives, librarians had departed from their original profession of faith in education and the library attempted to be all things to all people and did not succeed in any one activity.[67] Several librarians proposed that a rational purpose and a program of effective service would depend upon librarians understanding the role of the public library in society,[68] becoming thoroughly conscious of what they were trying to do, understanding why they were doing it, and then defining library objectives more sharply and making them primarily educational.[69]

In 1938, a more extensive statement of aims was formulated in "A National Plan for Libraries." In this document, adopted by the ALA Council, it was stated that the objectives of the public library were:

. . . to assemble and preserve books and related materials in organized collections and, through stimulation and guidance, to promote their use, to the end that children, young people, men, and women may have opportunity and encouragement:

To educate themselves continuously

To aid in the advancement of knowledge

To improve their capacity for appreciation and production in cultural fields

To improve their ability to participate usefully in activities in which they are involved as citizens

To equip themselves, and keep themselves equipped, for efficient activity in useful occupations and practical affairs

To keep abreast of progress in the sciences and other fields of knowledge

To maintain the precious heritage of freedom of expression and a constructively critical attitude toward all public issues

To make such use of leisure time as will promote personal happiness and social well-being.[70]

Although this statement of objectives was more specific than the one formulated in 1933, it was criticized as being too diffuse. One collection of library books, said Clarence E. Sherman, Librarian of the Providence (Rhode Island) Public Library, could not serve all the diverse needs and interests of a community. The continuing struggle and the subsequent failure in trying to satisfy all readers, he said, was "one reason why public libraries have not advanced too successfully in adult education. They are too busy along other lines to try seriously."[71] In 1940, Cecil McHale, of the University of Michigan Library School, suggested that in order "to prevent scattering and possible dissipation of energies," librarians should not continue to be "all things to all men." Instead, he said, they should determine the type of service the library could render better than any other agency, then map out a plan of action, concentrate on selected objectives, and pay serious attention to measuring and appraising results.[72]

The 1933 and 1938 statements of objectives marked the beginning of an intensive appraisal of the aims and services of public libraries. These statements stimulated much thought, discussion, and controversy. They were instrumental in helping librarians make sharper distinctions between essential and nonessential services; they established an important precedent and provided the basis for later and more extensive formulations of objectives; and they set forth an explicit statement of the public library's educational responsibility: to provide the materials, stimulation, and personal guidance for adults to educate themselves continuously.

Critics and Defenders of Library Adult Education

Most of the controversy about library adult education in the 1920's and 1930's was centered on the role of the public library in community adult education and the methods libraries used to provide educational services for adults.

Educational Role

The interpretation of the library's educational role during this period ranged from the conservative—"We should circulate books of educational value"—to the extreme liberal—"We should help to make the library the major agency of adult education." The various interpretations of this role can be delineated in five major categories:

1. To collect, preserve, and circulate books
2. To make books readily accessible
3. To cooperate with and to supplement the work of other adult educational agencies
4. To provide the type of educational service that the library is best qualified to offer
5. To become the major agency of adult education

Harry M. Lydenberg, Librarian of the New York (City) Public Library, who in 1933 was president of the American Library Association, maintained that "if we library workers view ourselves and our work in proper perspective, we must realize that we are not educators but rather the caretakers of important instruments of education."[73] In a similar vein, Robert A. Miller, a young library assistant, pointed out that the public library was only one agency for the distribution of books. Raising the question of the public library's proper place in the distributive scheme, Miller suggested that even though librarians glorified the library as an "educative force," the library's "main business is distributing books," and its proper role was to serve as a place of "mediation for books and reader."[74]

Another conception of the library's educational role was that all good library work was adult education. Lyman L. Bryson, the prominent adult educator, expressed the belief held by many librarians that

> ... if one accepts, as I do, the concept of the librarian as primarily an
> adult educator, and the concept of adult education as primarily an
> individual's search after the satisfactions of his own soul, most of what
> librarians and libraries can do will always be the building up of those
> possibilities that put persons in reach of books.[75]

A moderate position relating to the library's educational role was stated in "A National Plan for Libraries." This statement, which represented the thinking of many of the leaders of the library profession, affirmed:

> Library service is a social enterprise participating and cooperating
> with all other agencies and forces concerned with the welfare and progress
> of humanity. . . . A system of libraries which will serve these ends
> would seem to be, with our public school system, the minimum cultural
> equipment necessary for civilized living in America.[76]

The document further pointed out that the public library's specific educational role consisted of the provision of leadership and service by "cooperating with other educational agencies, supplementing their educational offerings with reading suggestions, and promoting the use of such agencies as a supplement to its own service."[77]

Louis R. Wilson, Dean of the Graduate Library School at the University of Chicago in 1936, pointed out that the public library could play an important role in adult education if it would concentrate "on the services it alone could offer."[78] Marshall Dimock, who had similar views, noted that the educational role of each public library was different. "The public library," he said,

> should accommodate those who know what they want, and, in addition,
> render service, plus guidance and encouragement, to those who need

encouragement. In its collaborative work with educational institutions and adult education movements the library role deserves to be called nothing short of promotional. In general, I believe that an aggressive, educational philosophy is the best. If the objective can be obtained by the institution's serving in an ancillary position, well and good; if not, then librarians should build their organizations for aggressive action.[79]

In 1938, Alvin Johnson, the distinguished educator, made an appraisal of the public library as an educational institution.[80] His report was prepared at the request of the American Association of Adult Education and was made possible by a grant from the Carnegie Corporation of New York. On the basis of an analysis of existing library services, Johnson asserted that "pure librarianship"—the process of collecting and distributing books without any regard to the influence they exerted—was not educational in character. All "good" library work was not adult education.

The most appropriate educational role for the library, Johnson contended, was a bold and active one. "The best possibility is to develop the public library into a permanent center of adult education, informally, a people's university." The justification for this role, in Johnson's view, was that the public library "has, as a first requisite in the adult education field, control of the supply of books. And books . . . contain the better part of the essentials of adult education."[81] Johnson's report stirred up much thought and discussion during the late 1930's and the early 1940's. The report is still useful; it stands today as the most comprehensive analysis of the public library's educational responsibility.

Of the various conceptions on the library's educational role, the one stated in "A National Plan for Libraries" was the most widely accepted by librarians, primarily because it was a moderate position representing a balance among the extreme views. Most of the positions taken on the library's educational role were assumed by persons actively concerned with the advancement of library adult education. This, however, was not the case in the controversy about the methods librarians used in providing adult educational services.

Educational Methods

The Commission on the Library and Adult Education recommended in 1926 the provision of person-to-person advisory service as the library's unique opportunity in adult education.[82] To some librarians the term "adult education" had the connotation of schooling and formal instruction, and "readers' advisory service" suggested to others that librarians were to engage in teaching. For those who believed that the public library of 1928 was departing from its regular activities and encroaching on the work of the schools, Matthew S. Dudgeon, the executive assistant to the ALA Board on the Library and Adult Education, stated: "I want to reassure you, if any of you are uneasy, that we have no thought of trying to change libraries into schoolhouses or to make over librarians into school teachers."[83] But some of the leaders of the profession were not convinced. In November, 1928, John Cotton Dana, Librarian of the Newark (New Jersey) Free Public Library, maintained:

> No library has a staff large enough to spare more than a few minutes
> each day to the special demands of each of a few inquirers. To do what the
> shibboleth "Adult Education," as we are now interpreting it, asks us to
> do, that is, to act as guides and teachers to all the adults we
> can persuade to come and ask us what they should read, and how, and
> to quiz them on their progress and advise them from day to day—all that
> is quite impossible.[84]

At the first ALA Institute on the Library and Adult Education in 1929, Judson T. Jennings, who was chairman of the ALA Commission on the Library and Adult Education, answered Dana. The function of the library in adult education, Jennings said, was not "that of the teacher, but rather that of the helper and adviser, and the program of adult education is based on the voluntary effort and interest of those who seek its service."[85] The same year, Arthur E. Bostwick, Librarian of the St. Louis Public Library, helped to clarify the issue by pointing out the difference between the function of the school and the function of the library. Although some librarians, he granted, were inclined to adopt the terminology of the school and the college in connection with readers' advisory service, they should understand that the function of the school was to teach, while the function of the library was to give assistance in learning. The teacher was in a position of authority, and the readers' adviser in a library was not; the latter performed a service to the public and was a servant rather than a teacher.[86] By 1935, the controversy about methods shifted to the question: Should librarians limit their adult education service to readers' guidance, or should they diversify their efforts and adopt some of the new educational methods being used in work with adult groups?

Between 1935 and 1938, the members of the ALA Adult Education Board and the ALA Adult Education Roundtable maintained that individual reading guidance was the library's primary method in adult education but affirmed that other methods, including the sponsorship of discussion groups, were also appropriate and should be utilized when needed. In 1935, Ernestine Rose, who was serving as chairman of the Adult Education Committee of the New York Library Association, proposed for the Association that a library could implement its educational objective by providing "educational activities under library auspices when desirable and feasible."[87]

At the University of Chicago's 1936 annual Library Institute, Edward

S. Robinson, Yale psychologist, suggested that if a librarian conceived of library books as instruments rather than as ends of the educational process, then "he will not hesitate to bring within sponsorship of the library any type of activity which will aid in the attainment of that enlargement and refinement of experience which is the ultimate aim of all educational endeavor."[88] Similarly, in 1938, the members of the ALA Adult Education Board stated that "there is little we can dispense in the way of approved methods, recipes, and formulae, as a medical information bureau. We feel that any tendency to codify or crystallize various techniques for adult education is distinctly dangerous."[89]

The practice of using more than one method to implement the library's educational objective had gained further acceptance by 1939. In "A National Plan for Libraries," the ALA committee appointed to draft this statement recommended that the library, "as an indispensable agency for education," provide

not only the materials but also the skilled personal advice and counseling
necessary to effective self-study. The library must perfect and extend
its advisory personnel and service. Because some kind of after-use of what
one reads is needed to make it one's own, the library should foster
formal and informal discussion among readers, and aid in any other
practical way to complete the educational process which
begins with reading.[90]

Several months later, Alice M. Farquhar, readers' adviser of the Chicago Public Library, suggested a wider perspective concerning the use of methods. Service to the individual, she maintained, was of first importance, but there was danger of "looking upon readers' advisory service as the only library adult education." The librarian should provide service to groups, be thoroughly familiar with developments in the whole field of adult education, and, when necessary, be "an active agent of adult education, sponsoring and inaugurating varying kinds of educational activities when it seems to be the job of no one else to do so, and offering library space for such activities."[91]

An even broader view of the methodology of library adult education was presented by John Chancellor, who concluded that librarians had been

too much concerned with finding a method for adult education in libraries
which could be codified as certain library techniques are; we
have tended too much toward making it a specialty, toward
departmentalizing it. We need now to think of involving the whole
library, putting a motive of informal education into all library planning
and practice, into book selection, cataloging, reference, desk
work and publicity; so that not one but all staff members will get a
vision of the great opportunity and challenge to serve better the new
inquisitiveness in people today, to understand themselves
and their world.[92]

Some of the factors of the 1920's and 1930's that had an influence upon the methodology and content of adult educational services of public libraries were:

Educational level. The increase in the educational level of the population created a wider audience of serious readers

Leisure time. The decrease in the average work week from 51.1 hours in 1920 to 40.1 hours in 1940 made it possible for more working adults to use the library

Adult educational movement. As the number of agencies and facilities for the education for adults multiplied during the 1920's and 1930's, the use of the public library by adults for educational purposes increased

Mass communications. With the serialization of new novels in magazines, the growth of rental libraries and book clubs, the increase in the number of radios in use (13 million in 1930 and 51 million in 1940), and the growth in the average weekly attendance at motion picture theaters (40 million a week in 1920 and 80 million a week in 1940), the need for public libraries to provide recreational services gradually decreased; therefore, more staff time and money could be allocated to the provision of educational services

Depression. During the Depression, the significance and comparative value of libraries to society were studied, the services of libraries were subjected to close scrutiny, and, as a result, librarians became more aware of their responsibility to identify the library with the needs and problems of society

Educational advances. As a result of the pedagogic recognition of individual differences and disparate capacities of children, librarians became more aware of the pluralistic nature of their clientele and began to give more attention to the different reading levels of adults

To sum up, between 1926 and 1940, a relatively small number of public libraries had full-time staff to provide organized programs of readers' advisory service. But during this period the majority of public librarians had accepted the appropriateness of providing this service. Also, a very small minority of librarians thought that they should provide service both to individuals and to groups.

The quality of library adult education during this period varied. Some librarians were deeply concerned about the effect of their educational efforts, while other librarians were only slightly concerned. The former consisted of a core of serious adult educators; the latter provided educational service either because it seemed the thing to do or because of its publicity value. The librarians who took an active part in library adult education were, at times, likely to exaggerate their accomplishments, and the critics of library adult education often underestimated the value of this phase of library work.

Lacking a unifying philosophy, focusing frequently on means rather than on ends, and being guided at times not by rational thinking but by enthusiasm, library adult education had not yet come of age. Nevertheless, between the end of World War I and the beginning of World War II, genuine educational effort characterized the work of a number of public libraries, and adult educational services through libraries became more organized, more comprehensive, and more effective.

The work of the American Library Association and particularly the efforts of creative pioneers—such as Judson T. Jennings, Miriam Tompkins, Jennie Flexner, and John Chancellor—helped librarians become more aware of adult education as a main responsibility of the library. The various educational projects of the Association stressed the importance of serving the individual reader in search of self-education and, in general, resulted in the growth and refinement of readers' advisory service.

Strengthening Democracy

1941–1956

Public librarians, during the 1940's and the first half of the 1950's, were concerned with ideas and with the various ways, in addition to print, that could be used to communicate ideas. During and immediately following World War II, they placed major emphasis on promoting enlightened citizenship and assisting in the realization of democratic ideals. These interests eventually culminated in educational experiments that permanently enriched the practice of library adult education.

Preservation and Improvement of American Democracy

The part that books could play in preparation for military defense and in the advancement of the war was of concern to librarians during the first half of the 1940's. Then, at the close of World War II, they turned their attention to the task of creating an enlightened citizenry and strengthening freedom of expression and inquiry.

Wartime Activities

In 1941, the American Library Association prepared a policy statement, adopted by the ALA Council, which emphasized the responsibility of every library to furnish citizens with an unbiased knowledge of current events, and the duty of every librarian to promote understanding of the principles on which the United States form of government was based.[1] In response, librarians provided materials to aid adults in comprehending the problems of war and peace, supplied technical books to meet the needs of workers in defense industries, furnished information about civil defense, and established war information centers, many of which were given official designation by the government.[2] They assisted, in 1942 and 1943, in the Victory Book Campaign—a project to collect books for the armed forces to supplement the existing collections provided by the Army and Navy. Libraries, serving as receiving and sorting centers, collected more than 17 million volumes in two successive book drives.[3]

In 1944, librarians began to plan for postwar developments in library service. Conferences were held to determine ways that libraries could assist in the readjustment of veterans returning to civilian life, and workshops were organized to discuss the acquisition of books that would be needed when normal library service was resumed.

Postwar Activities

With the close of the war came the effort to promote enlightened citizenship and to strengthen freedom of expression and inquiry. In 1945, Carl Vitz, Librarian of the Cincinnati Public Library and then President of the American Library Association, pointed out the role of books in building a secure peace and a stable social order. Citizens trained in the requirements of peace, he emphasized, were as necessary in the postwar world as were trained soldiers during the war.[4] To help in the creation of a community of thinking citizens, holding opinions independently gained, was a principal task of librarians. In an attempt to exert an influence on public opinion, the American Library Association initiated two civic education programs, designed to provide opportunities for adults to examine divergent points of view on local, national, and international affairs. The first was the "Great Issues" program, organized in 1948 for the purpose of stimulating reading and discussion on such problems as inflation, world government, management-labor relations, the United States and Russia, and civil rights.[5] The second was the ALA American Heritage Project, begun in 1951, which was made possible by a grant from the Fund for Adult Education. The purpose of this project was to assist libraries throughout the United States in providing opportunities for adults to discuss the political, social, and economic problems of the day in the light of the basic documents, ideas, and experiences which constituted the American heritage.[6]

In 1948, the members of the American Library Association became concerned about restrictions on freedom of expression and inquiry. One of the major problems facing the United States in the years between 1948 and 1954 was the conflict between individual freedom and national security. As a result of the "cold war" between the United States and Russia, tensions in this country increased, and various types of restrictive measures were adopted to protect the nation's security in a time of crisis. It was a period characterized by congressional investigations; loyalty programs for federal, state, and city government employees; discussions and decisions in respect to academic freedom in public and private institutions of higher learning; and censorship of books in schools, colleges, and public and governmental libraries.

The American Library Association, in resisting attempts to limit freedom of expression and especially in trying to prevent censorship, advocated an unrestricted and uncensored flow of fact and opinion within the United States and among nations. At the 1948 ALA Conference, the members of the ALA Council reaffirmed and strengthened the Library Bill of Rights, a policy statement which set forth basic principles concerning the free access to ideas and information,[7] and adopted a resolution condemning loyalty investigations in libraries.[8] Other attempts to encourage free inquiry included the first ALA Intellectual Freedom Institute in 1952, followed by a second in 1953, and the ALA Conference program in 1954, "Knowledge—A Free People's Secret Strength."[9]

In addition to their efforts directed toward strengthening national conceptions of citizenship and freedom, public librarians of this period devoted time and effort to the planning and passage of the Library Services Act, designed to bring library service to rural areas; acquiring and circulating audio-visual materials (films, slides, filmstrips, recordings, and framed pictures); utilizing television for educational and publicity purposes; and clarifying library objectives.

Clarifying Public Library Objectives

During the 1940's and 1950's there was much discussion about the essential aims and changing goals of the American public library. Three major attempts were made to clarify public library objectives; the results of these efforts were described in *Post-War Standards for Public Libraries* (1943); the summary volume of the Public Library Inquiry, *The Public Library in the United States* (1950); and *Public Library Service* (1956), each of which will be discussed more fully below.

Post-War Standards for Public Libraries

At the request of the National Resources Planning Board, the American Library Association appointed a committee in 1942 to formulate standards for public libraries which would serve as a guide to library development during the postwar period. Under the chairmanship of Carleton B. Joeckel, Dean of the Graduate Library School at the University of Chicago, the ALA Committee on Post-War Planning prepared a comprehensive statement of library aims and standards. This statement, *Post-War Standards for Public Libraries,* was published in 1943.[10]

In this report, the members of the ALA Committee on Post-War Planning stated that, although the aims of public libraries had "almost always been broad and diffused" and "succinct codification" was difficult, the objectives of the American public library might be "codified by the use of five convenient word symbols: (1) education, (2) information, (3) aesthetic appreciation, (4) research, and (5) recreation." Recognizing that these terms were not mutually exclusive and that people who used public libraries for the purposes stated could not be sharply differentiated, the members of the committee affirmed that "the central idea symbolized by each of these five terms is sufficiently clear to warrant its use as a short-cut designation of a library objective."[11]

The report recommended that public libraries, in carrying out these objectives, should avoid "the dangers of too great diffusion of effort" by careful selection of those functions that "the library is best fitted to perform." It suggested that particular emphasis should be placed on the provision of educational and informational services:

> Among these strategic areas for the concentration of public library effort,
> perhaps the most important is the field of adult education. If it is true that
> "the future of democracy depends in a genuine sense upon adult
> education," the public library should point its efforts more directly
> toward this important area of service. Whether the library is a leader
> or a follower in the adult education program, its services as "a people's
> university" should be continuously strengthened. Another area of
> concentration within the field of adult education is the role of the public
> library as a focal point for service to the citizen in the examination
> of the problems of public affairs. Here also the position of the library is
> strategically fortunate. The potentialities of the public library as a
> center of facts and figures for the citizen should be fully exploited in
> the post-war period.[12]

The objectives set forth in *Post-War Standards for Public Libraries,* and the recommendations concerning the emphasis to be placed on these objectives, were considered at length during the next five years. Discussions ranged from debates on "how librarians can live with these objectives" to disagreements concerning both the number of recommended library objectives and the amount of emphasis to be given to each. In 1946, Cyril O. Houle, then Dean of University College, the University of Chicago, commented on the five objectives of public libraries and pointed out that it was impossible "to separate any one of these functions from the other." Nevertheless, he suggested that many librarians act as though each objective should be "sought by some part of the library rather than by the whole agency," while others "concentrate on only one objective, ignoring the others." By means of an analogy to the multipurpose dams of the Tennessee Valley Authority, Houle identified the practical conditions that librarians faced in implementing library objectives:

> Each dam has not one but several functions, among which are the
> production of power, the prevention of floods, and the provision
> of navigation. It will be readily recognized that each of these functions
> to some extent negates the others. For purposes of power, for example, it

is desirable to have a large amount of water behind the dam so that continuous energy will be assured. For purposes of flood control, on the other hand, it is desirable to have as little water behind the dam as possible so that the reservoir may be free to catch and hold any excessive flow from the hills. In terms of practical administration, some balance must be struck between these competing purposes which will assure, as well, that other goals will also be served. It is impossible to achieve each in the fullest degree so long as the other exists.[13]

In 1946, Joseph L. Wheeler, who had recently retired from the librarianship of the Enoch Pratt Free Library of Baltimore, maintained that the public library had a responsibility not for five but for three objectives: "Librarianship is concerned primarily with books and other materials, their discovery, selection, preparation, and with increasing emphasis, their full utilization, by all classes and individuals who have the intelligence to learn and the gumption to seek information, recreation, or self-development from them."[14] The following year, Herbert Goldhor, Professor of Library Science at the University of Illinois Library School, suggested that, with the concentration on work with adults and with the expansion of school libraries for children, it was likely that less emphasis would be placed "on the recreational and research functions" and more emphasis "on the informational and educational functions."[15] In terms of future library aims, Goldhor's prediction was valid, as was evidenced in the next attempt to clarify library objectives.

Public Library Inquiry

The most comprehensive study of public library objectives was the Public Library Inquiry, undertaken in 1947 by the American Library Association and the Social Science Research Council and made possible by a grant from the Carnegie Corporation of New York. This landmark study was carried out by a group of nonlibrarians (trained in one or another of the social sciences) under the direction of Robert D. Leigh, who served as chairman of the Public Library Inquiry. It examined public library objectives, programs, structure, operations, and problems. The survey and final volume of the Inquiry report, *The Public Library in the United States* by Robert D. Leigh, was published in 1950.

On the basis of an extensive appraisal in sociological, cultural, and human terms of the extent "to which librarians are achieving their objectives," and "an assessment of the public library's actual and potential contribution to American society," the Inquiry report recommended that the objectives of the public library should be "to serve the community as a general center of reliable information and to provide opportunity and encouragement for people of all ages to educate themselves continuously."[16]

Unlike previous statements of library objectives, the Inquiry report provided a rationale for its recommendations. In connection with the educational objective, the report stated that the public library was not the "people's university," but an institution that provided the means of self-education to a small but significant portion of the population. The library's function, according to the report, was to serve that group of adults "whose interest, will, and ability" led them to seek personal enrichment and enlightenment. Although the library might seek to enlarge this "natural library audience," the evidence of the Inquiry report substantiated the conclusion that the process of enlargement was slow, "requiring intensive efforts and not producing numerically spectacular results." Therefore, the report recommended that the major efforts of public libraries should be directed toward providing adequate informational and educational services to this small but select group of natural library users. If this was done, it was suggested, a social contribution "much greater than the gross numbers involved" would result.[17]

This recommendation, however, was not acceptable to all librarians. It was questioned by some advocates[18] as well as by some critics[19] of library adult education. The discussion evoked was centered primarily on what most librarians considered to be the library's two principal objectives: education and recreation.

The findings and recommendations of the Public Library Inquiry stimulated widespread discussion; one of the significant outcomes of this discussion was the further attention given to defining the library's educational objective more precisely. In 1950, Cyril O. Houle discussed the work of the library in relation to two concepts of education: random experience and purposeful experience in which a systematic and deliberate attempt to learn or to teach was present. In commenting on the value of conscious goals in education, Houle said that

> . . . some adult educators prefer to use the term "education" as signifying
> not all experience but only that more direct kind which is undertaken
> with a desire to learn or a desire to teach. If we were to draw a large circle
> and label it "experience" we would need to draw a smaller circle within
> the larger and call it "education." In this case the incidental learning
> products of the experience which is not undertaken for purposes
> of education might be called "conditioning" or some other term. But
> whatever words we use, we are not merely playing with words. There is a
> real and substantial difference between experience which is directed
> toward the learning of new skills, knowledge, understanding,
> attitudes, or appreciations and that which is not.[20]

Similarly, Bernard Berelson, Dean of the Graduate Library School of the University of Chicago, claimed that education, to some librarians,

> . . . is practically synonymous with the circulation of nonfiction,
> while others feel that the library satisfies its educational objective by
> supplying books such as *Forever Amber* to people who will thereby learn

something about the court of Charles II. It should be clear that the objective of "education" is not meant to mean either of these. But if one defines education as involving both (a) ethical, moral, and intellectual improvement of some magnitude and (b) purposeful and systematic activity, then one comes a little closer to a solid meaning which can serve as a guide for library action.[21]

Further clarification of the library's educational objective was achieved in 1954 at the Allerton Park Conference, which was attended by thirty-eight directors and faculty members of university library schools and adult education departments and by administrators of small, medium, and large libraries. A consensus definition of library adult education was formulated:

> . . . those library activities for adult individuals and groups which form a
> part of the total educational process and which are marked by a defined
> goal, derived from an analysis of needs or interests. These activities aim at
> a continuing cumulative educational experience for those who participate,
> require special planning and organization, and may be originated by
> the library or by a request from the individuals or groups concerned.[22]

Much of the controversy about the Public Library Inquiry centered on its omission of the recreational objective. In commenting on the reasons why this objective was not recommended, Robert Leigh said that the Inquiry report

> . . . does not imply that furnishing materials for entertainment, relaxation,
> and escape is unimportant in our society, but only that the commercial
> media are motivated and well-equipped to perform this function
> and that there are other social needs to which the commercial media
> do not minister as adequately as the library can.[23]

In relating this recommendation to current library practice, Ralph Munn, Director of the Carnegie Library of Pittsburgh, who apparently agreed with the recommendation, asked:

> . . . should public libraries conclude that the other media are taking over
> the entertainment field and that libraries need no longer supply
> mystery and detective stories, love and romance novels, adventure
> and western stories, best-selling novels of no distinction, and all
> comparable books of nonfiction—in short, books which are of little value
> except as entertainment? Apparently a large number of librarians
> are not yet ready to abandon the entertainment field.[24]

The clear-cut distinction between education and recreation made in the report of the Public Library Inquiry was disturbing to some librarians. In 1950, Lowell Martin, then Associate Dean of the School of Library Service, Columbia University, suggested that, in terms of current public library practice, the emphasis "falls on the side of the supplier," while the emphasis in the literature is on the "educational function of the agency." We seem, said Martin, to have the desire "to be both more popular and more purposeful at one and the same time. While these two aims are not necessarily antithetical, they can work at cross purposes."[25]

In 1955, Martin, then Dean of the Graduate School of Library Service at Rutgers University, concluded that

> . . . the great discussion of these years has presumably been about purpose, from Learned to Leigh, with many a lesser effort between. But it often loses the straight path of purpose to turn into the byway, on one side, of how people achieve purpose (whether through education or recreation), and, on the other side, of how libraries contribute to purpose (whether by individual or group methods). Both byways lead far from the point at issue. After these discussions, the practicing librarian finds himself as far as ever from a clear basis for action. He may even show signs of a split personality, between the calls to provide education and to serve his community. No respectable librarian would admit these days to giving people only what they want; no sound librarian would in practice give the people what they do not want.[26]

Martin's point of view represented the thinking of a considerable number of librarians, and the next official statement of library aims recommended, not two, but three objectives.

Public Library Service

In 1956, the American Library Association published *Public Library Service: A Guide to Evaluation, with Minimum Standards*. This statement of principles, prepared by the ALA Co-ordinating Committee on Revision of Public Library Standards under the chairmanship of Lowell A. Martin, provided a guide for assessing library service and formulating plans for improvement. The document, which was officially adopted by the ALA Council, recommended that the objectives of public libraries should be: education ("to facilitate informal self-education of all people in the community"), information ("to meet the informational needs of all"), and recreation ("to encourage wholesome recreation and constructive use of leisure time").[27]

Five objectives and three goals[28] were recommended in *Post-War Standards for Public Libraries;* two objectives and two goals in the summary volume of the Public Library Inquiry; and three objectives in *Public Library Service.* The latter statement of objectives was clearer and more specific than the earlier ones. Moreover, it represented a major step forward in the formulation of library objectives. An examination of *Public Library Service* reveals that the members of the Committee who prepared this statement emphasized the distinction between broad institutional objectives and specific operational goals—an important distinction that was not made in the earlier ALA statements of library objectives.

Educational Role of the Library

Three markedly different concepts of the library's educational role were prevalent during the 1940's and 1950's. Some librarians claimed that the public library should concentrate on providing services for adult educational activities maintained by other organizations and groups in the community. Other librarians held the view that the public library should provide active adult educational programs of its own, which would demonstrate the library's unique educational role and result in recognition of the library as an important educational agency. Still other librarians maintained that the public library should provide the educational services it was best qualified to offer in relation to the needs and resources of the community.

Services to Other Organizations

The most widely accepted role of the library in adult education, as judged in terms of actual practice,[29] was to provide auxiliary services for the educational programs of other organizations. These library services included: supplying books to adult students engaged in study under other auspices, such as adult education programs of the agricultural extension service and the adult education division of public schools, colleges, and universities; assisting community groups in planning programs and in locating suitable program materials and resources; and supporting the educational activities of other organizations by providing information about the adult educational opportunities available in the community. This position, which might be called that of the "auxiliarists," was questioned by a small number of librarians who maintained that the library's primary educational role was to serve as an agency of self-education for adults who wished to continue their education through reading. R. N. O'Reilly, an Irish librarian and student of the American public library, pointed out in 1947 that the public library could perform an important educational service without being complementary to any particular educational institution, or even without other educational institutions at all, because all that was "required is that individuals should have the desire to understand something that can be learned from books or to experience something that can be found in good literature; educational institutions do but nurture [sic] these educational desires."[30]

Active Adult Educational Programs

A second view of the library's educational role was that the public library should become a general agency of out-of-school education. This position, which was proclaimed by a relatively small but articulate group of librarians during the 1940's and early 1950's, assumed that education took place primarily in a group situation. Therefore, a public library, by sponsoring its own program (lectures, discussion groups, study clubs, concerts, and various types of workshops), could assume a more vital role in community adult education.

In 1943, the ALA Committee on Post-War Planning stated that, since the American public library could "lead in informal education" and become the people's university, each library, therefore, should develop an active program of adult education. Libraries serving a population of 25,000 and over should have specialists to provide guidance to individuals and groups. Large libraries should have a corps of reading specialists; field representatives to work with various civic, labor, and other community groups; and library leaders and organizers of discussion groups, study clubs, and film forums.[31]

Five years later, a second report of this committee was issued[32] in which it was stated that the public library was

> . . . one of the few institutions that provide educational service to adults
> as a central function rather than as an appendage to other tasks.
> Schools are primarily for children, churches for religion, labor unions
> for economic betterment. But the public library is the major agency
> of enlightenment for adults. And it is a source of recorded experience for
> children as they grow into adulthood. The public library is one of the
> few agencies that exist to serve their constituents and not to advance a
> cause or sell a product.
> . . . .
> The public library is potentially an essential unit in the American
> educational system. In isolated instances it has played a crucial role in the
> life of the community. In many instances it has in its day-to-day
> performance quietly aided the search for understanding. It comes closer
> than any other institution to being the capstone of our educational system.[33]

This position, which was held by some of the leaders of the library profession, was based on the belief that the public library, in order to assume a major role in community adult education, should offer a variety of educational services to promote adult learning.

Educational Services Related to Community Needs

A third point of view, held by a very small minority of librarians during the 1940's and the first half of the 1950's,[34] became more widely accepted in 1956, when the ALA's *Public Library Service* was published and the ALA Library-Community Project[35] was getting under way. This concept of the library's educational role was that the public library, as a community institution, should continuously study its community in order to know people, groups, and institutions thoroughly; maintain close contact with other agencies; be informed of the activities of these agencies; and design the library's adult educational program in relation to the educational needs of the community, the programs and services offered by other agencies, and the library's resources and the special skills of the library staff.[36]

Of the libraries that provided adult educational services during this period, most of the small and some of the medium-sized ones performed an auxiliary educational role, while most of the large and a few of the medium-sized ones assumed what was called an "active" educational role. By 1956, however, some librarians began to reexamine their adult educational services in relation to community needs and resources. This marked the beginning of the next phase in the evolution of the library's educational role. Between 1956 and 1960, the library's educational work was gradually integrated into the general area of "adult services," which consisted of library services for the continuing educational, recreational, and cultural development of adults.

Educational Services

The educational services provided by the public libraries of this period were directed toward three major goals: civic enlightenment, vocational improvement, and personal development. The major emphasis throughout the 1940's and the first half of the 1950's was on civic enlightenment: helping individuals to enlarge their understanding of the problems of war and of building a durable peace, and assisting them in acquiring a knowledge of the meaning of democracy.[37] From 1941 to 1950, librarians were also concerned with vocational improvement: providing information and services to the men and women who worked in defense industries during the war, and assisting the defense worker and the returned veteran with problems of occupational adjustment immediately after the war.[38] Between 1950 and 1956, librarians turned some of their attention to personal development: helping individuals to extend their cultural background, satisfy avocational interests, and further personal self-realization.[39]

Public libraries of the 1940's and 1950's provided *services* to individuals, adult education agencies, and community groups and sponsored their own adult educational *programs*. During the war (1941–1945), readers' advisory service in some libraries was provided by various members of the professional staff, and special emphasis was placed on the provision of services and programs for groups of adults. There were several reasons for this shift of emphasis. First, readers' guidance, provided by a single staff member or by a special staff, was the most costly of all library services. Second, there was a shortage of professional librarians during the war years and also during the immediate postwar period. Third, public libraries could provide more educational services to more people by working with groups than by serving individuals through a readers' advisory program. Fourth, research findings relating to group dynamics and the experimentation in work with small groups during the 1940's helped to stimulate interest among librarians in group services and programs. Despite the growing emphasis on working with groups, library service to individuals was not completely forgotten.

Services to Individuals

During this period, educational services to individual readers included supplying books of educational value, providing personal assistance, utilizing techniques to stimulate interest in good books, and providing readers' advisory service. The selection of books for adult learning, suggested R. N. O'Reilly, was "the greatest educational task of the librarian."[40] The next step was to get books of this type used. To achieve this purpose, the majority of public librarians of this period attempted to stimulate an interest in good books by means of exhibits, displays, book talks, and book lists.[41]

Readers' advisory service, furnished by a special staff, was provided in the 1940's and 1950's in only about ten libraries, while in 1935 there had been sixty-three readers' advisers in forty-four public libraries of varying sizes. Outstanding advisory programs, however, were provided throughout the 1940's and 1950's by the public libraries of New York City, Detroit, and Cincinnati. Lowell Martin, in commenting on the reduction in the number of librarians assigned specifically to providing readers' advisory service and on the dispersal of this responsibility among more members of the library staff, suggested that "sharing of the guidance responsibility has much to be said for it, for all librarians are engaged in the facilitation of reading, but it may be that the sharing occurred too soon, before the spirit of individual guidance was strong enough and its methods developed enough to carry over into a less dedicated group."[42]

Group Services and Programs

What is often called "group work" in public libraries may be divided into two main types: (1) services to adult educational agencies and to community groups and (2) library-sponsored group programs. Services to adult educational agencies in this period included the preparation of library exhibits and displays to call attention to the programs and courses of adult educational agencies; the supplying of printed materials for adult students; and, in some instances, the furnishing of facilities for classes to meet. An outstanding example of this latter service was the provision of the rooms in a number of New York Public Library branches as classrooms by the City College of New York.

Library services to community groups—labor organizations, women's study clubs, church groups, parents groups, men's clubs, and other voluntary associations—led to closer coordination of community programs and greater participation by libraries in the planning of community activities. In 1944, the members of the ALA Adult Education Board noted: "Beginning with the emphasis on individual study, we progressed to group work and discussion, and now we speak more of learning by doing, especially by working cooperatively on community problems."[43] The services rendered to community groups by the majority of public libraries during the late 1940's and early 1950's were: the preparation of library exhibits and displays to publicize the programs and activities of these groups; the presentation of book talks; and the provision of advice in program planning.[44] Outstanding examples of these services were the book talks given by the staff of the Cuyahoga County (Ohio) Public Library and the program planning service of the Akron (Ohio) Public Library.

The major kinds of library-sponsored group programs of this period were varied book and audio-visual programs, discussion group programs, and program planning institutes. The book and audio-visual programs were presented, primarily by large libraries, by means of various methods (lecture, discussion forum, workshop, institute, panel discussion), based on the use of a variety of materials (books, pamphlets, and various forms of audio-visual materials), and centered on such subjects as civic and world affairs, family life, problems of the aging, music, literature, art, finance, and child care.[45] One of the most successful and large-scale programs of this type was the Atomic Energy Institute, developed in 1947 by the Enoch Pratt Free Library of Baltimore, for the purpose of disseminating knowledge about the atomic bomb and nuclear fission. This program, which was sponsored in cooperation with a number of community groups and agencies, was carried out by distributing 50,000 copies of a folder in which the program was described; preparing and distributing an equal number of copies of a book list called "You and the Atom"; supplying large quantities of the recommended books in the main library and its branches; providing special film, lecture, and discussion forum programs on the atom bomb; preparing an attractive and comprehensive exhibition on the subject in cooperation with Johns Hopkins University; and following up various activities of the Institute by making available an outline of suggestions for study, reading, and discussion in which the library offered its aid and cooperation.[46]

Other outstanding examples of this general type of program were: the Cleveland Public Library's series on problems of aging; the art and literature programs of the Seattle Public Library; the various programs for labor groups sponsored by the public libraries of Milwaukee, Akron, and New York City; the series of programs on "Crime and the Citizen" presented by the Enoch Pratt Free Library; the excellent programs on reading improvement provided by the public libraries of Detroit, Trenton (New Jersey), Brooklyn, and New York City; and some of the programs of small and medium-sized libraries that were made possible by the ALA Adult Education Subgrant Project.[47]

The second popular type of library group program of this period was the discussion group organized around specified readings, with all participants using the same source material as a point of focus. During the early 1940's, some librarians proposed that if reading were to make a contribution to personal development and civic understanding, the reader must have an opportunity to discuss what he read. The major premises of library-sponsored discussion programs were: while learning might be acquired by self-study, perceptiveness was enhanced and good judgment formed and nourished by discussion with others; adults were not likely to reach the upper levels of maturity in reading unless they had the stimulation of disciplined conversation and the opportunity to react thoughtfully to what they read; and discussion programs were effective means of encouraging purposeful reading and directing attention to writers and books that might not otherwise be read and appreciated.

In 1944, the ALA Adult Education Board issued a challenge to public librarians:

> Library programs must be keyed . . . to create thinking and discussion.
> . . . It is not enough to stand as an agency which on call can supply reading and information. The library must project its personnel and its
> books into the planning and thinking of the community.[48]

Library-sponsored discussion programs began to flourish in the period immediately following the close of World War II. Leadership in this type of program was first provided by the public libraries of Washington, D.C., and Chicago.

The Public Library of Washington, D.C., initiated its "Group Reading Program" in January, 1945, under the direction of Professor Scott Buchanan of St. John's College, with financial assistance from the Education Fund of Chicago. During the next three years of this program, some 1,500 adults enrolled in 120 groups and discussed full-length books by such writers as Plato, Freud, Emerson, Dewey, Veblen, Dreiser, and Farrell.[49]

In the fall of 1945, the Chicago Public Library, in cooperation with the University of Chicago, began offering Great Books seminars. Within a year, adults in thirty neighborhoods in and around Chicago were meeting in public libraries to discuss selections from the standard classics, based on a pattern of discussion adopted by Mortimer Adler and his associates at the University of Chicago.[50] In 1946, the University relinquished its control of the program to the Great Books Foundation; by 1949, Great Books discussion groups were organized in more than 200 cities, usually through libraries.

In 1948, the American Library Association initiated a civic education program called "Great Issues," designed to stimulate reading and discussion of the crucial problems facing the nation.[51] In 1950, the New York (City) Public Library developed a discussion program based on a variation of the "Great Issues" theme. This program, "Exploring the American Idea," led in 1951 to the development of the ALA American Heritage Project, the most extensive adult educational program ever undertaken by the public libraries of this country. Between 1951 and 1955, 1,474 American Heritage discussion groups were formed in thirty-three states, for the purpose of providing opportunities for men and women to meet together regularly and to discuss current political, social, and economic problems in the light of the basic documents, ideas, and experiences which constituted the American Heritage. During the four years of the Project, 28,476 adults participated in the program.[52]

The third and less-prevalent type of library-sponsored group activity of this period was the program planning institute. Provided as an aid for program chairmen of community groups and organizations, these institutes offered instruction in the fundamentals of good programming and the techniques of program presentation and furnished information on local resources and materials. The most widely acclaimed program planning institutes were those sponsored annually by the public libraries of Seattle, Detroit, Buffalo, Battle Creek (Michigan), Cuyahoga County (Ohio), and Artesia (New Mexico).[53]

Between 1946 and 1950, much progress had been made in the number and quality of the group services and programs provided by public libraries. In 1951, attention was given to determining the nature and scope of these services.

Assessment of Educational Services and Programs

Two attempts were made during the first half of the 1950's to obtain a more accurate picture of the type and extent of the adult educational activities of public libraries. The first, undertaken in 1951 and 1952, was concerned with surveying the educational activities of libraries in rural areas of the country.[54] In 1952 and 1953, a more extensive survey of the educational activities of public libraries located in communities of more than 2,500 population was conducted.[55]

In the survey of rural libraries, based on questionnaire responses received from 102 libraries, 58 percent of these libraries reported that they provided educational programs for adults directed toward civic, international, and economic understanding, with the greatest number of programs presented in the form of public meetings at which discussion and lectures were the most frequently used methods.[56] The more comprehensive study of the group services of public libraries, conducted in 1952 and 1953, was based on replies from 1,692 public libraries. It was found that 128 libraries, or 8 percent of the libraries responding to the questionnaire, were doing a great deal of adult education; 795, or 47 percent, were doing a medium amount; 769, or 45 percent, were doing little. The twelve chief educational services provided by these libraries, according to the survey, were:[57]

Service	Percent of Libraries
Exhibits and displays in the library	88
Book talks	67
Advice in program planning	65
Exhibits and displays outside the library	58
Participation in planning community programs	58
Publicizing of adult educational activities and programs of the community	54
Library programs on special subjects	50
Printed materials in duplicate quantity	50
Physical facilities	48
Information service on adult educational opportunities in the community	38
Library programs based on books	37
Information service about audio-visual materials	36

Some of the leaders of the profession, in observing the proliferation of adult educational services and programs of the public libraries of this period, expressed the belief that librarians were not justified in attempting to undertake everything that purported to be "educative."[58] Nevertheless, few of them, it was suggested, "seem to be able to resist the temptation to dabble" in adult education—an activity for which many of them "have no training and no talent."[59] This was evidenced by the fact that librarians often provided adult educational programs without having any clear-cut idea of the educational needs the program should meet, and that some of these programs were not really "educational," even with a broad interpretation of the term.[60] Moreover, it was maintained that many of these programs, despite widespread publicity, were actually "peripheral,"[61] "unconsidered sidelines,"[62] mere "appendages" to the library's main line of activity.[63]

Much of the controversy about library adult education centered on the use of methods and whether libraries should serve individuals or groups or both. Some librarians held the view that the library's first and only responsibility was to serve individuals.[64] Others suggested that librarians should serve both individuals and groups.[65] Still other librarians equated the group services and programs of libraries with a teaching function.[66]

Several leaders in the field thought that the individual *versus* group work argument among librarians was meaningless. The debate continued, they suggested, because the library concept of adult education was too narrow; what was not understood was that adult education was a way of working. Adult education should permeate all phases of library work, because it was concerned primarily with "the way in which librarians perform those activities they are already engaged in."[67]

During the 1940's and 1950's, many broad claims were made for adult educational service by enthusiasts, as well as much criticism of it by detractors. Most of the significant advances in the provision of this service, however, were due to the creative pioneers as well as to the constructive critics.

In summary, the major emphasis of the public libraries of this period was on assisting individuals and groups to acquire a knowledge of democratic principles and to form an enlightened opinion upon public affairs. In carrying out this purpose, some librarians thought that community and group contacts were more effective and more economical, particularly during wartime, than advisory service to individuals. This change of emphasis in respect to methodology was reflected in the 1954 ALA publication, *Adult Education Activities in Public Libraries,* which was a survey of the group services and programs of public libraries. The use of various means, such as lectures, forums, discussion groups, films, and television, was primarily an effort to stimulate and encourage the effective use of library resources. But librarians' acceptance of some of the newer educational methods and materials was gradual. In 1946, the majority of librarians were reluctant to accept leadership in working with groups. In 1953, library sponsorship of discussion groups and program planning institutes was fairly well established in the large libraries, but still not completely accepted as a library function in small and medium-sized libraries.

Two factors that had a major effect upon the growth and implementation of the adult educational services and programs of this period were:

1. *The ALA Adult Education Projects.* The greatest stimulus to library adult education of this period was the leadership that the American Library Association exercised through the various projects supported by grants from the Fund for Adult Education: American Heritage Project (1951–1955), Survey of Adult Education in Public Libraries (1952–1953), Adult Education Subgrant Project (1953–1954), and the Allerton Park Conference (1954).
2. *The Public Library Inquiry.* The Inquiry report helped to provide the library profession with a new focus and sense of direction, it recommended new and improved methods of operation, and it presented the first realistic picture of the status and potential of the American public library.

Moving Forward

1957–1964

Among the matters of concern to public librarians during the late 1950's and early 1960's were the implementing of public library standards by working together in developing library systems, securing federal assistance for strengthening public libraries, seeking a way to provide adequate service to students, and resolving the problem of free access to libraries.

Areas of Concern to Librarians

Two major historic events occurred in 1956: (1) the formulation of goals set forth in *Public Library Service* and (2) some provision toward the achievement of these goals, made possible by the passage of the Library Services Act.

Goals for Public Libraries

The 1956 standards, *Public Library Service,*[1] urged libraries to band together into systems, in order that small libraries in rural areas could have access to a wider range of resources. The assumptions underlying the systems approach were: an individual's library needs are in no way related to the size of the community in which he lives; persons such as teachers, engineers, and students need the same quality of library service regardless of whether they reside in a large city or a small town; and the small public library, organized and operated as an independent unit, usually cannot supply the range of books needed by its readers.[2]

The library systems concept, simply stated, means that by working together and sharing services and materials, libraries can better meet the needs of their users. The basic condition necessary for developing systems is voluntary cooperation. Although cooperation can take many forms, the intent is to get governmental units to work together to organize better and more extensive public library service.

The overall aim of library systems is to provide better library service in greater depth and on a quality level which few independent libraries outside major metropolitan cities can render. Some of the advantages in developing library systems may be: larger collections available to people in small as well as in large communities; centralized cataloging and processing; coordination of interlibrary loans; cooperative acquisition and use of books and other library materials; provision of special personnel such as subject specialists and adult services librarians available to all libraries in the system; less duplication of materials such as films, special collections, and reference materials; and better service to all of the people in the area by providing a way in which all persons are free to use the library located nearest to them.

State library associations responded to the 1956 standards in a variety of ways. In a number of states the standards were adopted as state standards; in others, public librarians agreed that they were too high and set about formulating lower interim standards based upon *Public Library Service* for use within their own areas while working toward achievement of the 1956 standards. In still other states, it was recognized that, although the public libraries in the state could not at that time meet the standards, the development of a long-range goal of upgrading according to a statewide plan (covering a period of five to ten years) could bring library service nearer to the accepted level recommended by the ALA standards.[3]

Federal Assistance
for Strengthening Public Libraries

In 1956, approximately 27 million people in the United States were without any local public library (90 percent of the 27 million people lived in rural areas), while another 53 million had inadequate service. The improvement of public library service, with emphasis on the development of library systems, received considerable impetus in 1957 when federal funds were made available to the states through the Library Services Act, which was the first federal program of assistance to public libraries.

The purpose of the Library Services Act was twofold. The manifest purpose was to bring library service to rural areas of less than 10,000 population which had no library service or inadequate or substandard service. The latent purpose was to stimulate the use of state and local funds for the improvement of library service through the use of federal funds. Between 1957 and 1963, the Library Services Act brought $42 million to the states, and local and state matching funds totaled more than $94 million.

During the first five years of the Library Services Act, the most popular programs begun by the various states were: demonstrations of library service in rural areas; the development and strengthening of county libraries; and the promotion of regional libraries. During the second phase of the Library Services Act (1961-66), which included authorization for federal funds to states and territories on a matching basis, major, though varying, emphasis was given to five types of programs: (1) the organization of county and multicounty library systems, including both short-term demonstrations and more permanent establishments; (2) centralized processing; (3) surveys of rural library services; (4) scholarship grants to prepare librarians for service in rural libraries; and (5) in-service training programs for rural librarians.

The Library Services Act accomplished much within a relatively short period of time. The two major accomplishments during the first seven years of the program were: (1) more than 40 million rural people were provided with new or improved public library services and (2) state funds for the development of public library service in rural areas were increased 100 percent between 1956 and 1963. Other advances included: local appropriations for rural libraries increased; new bookmobiles were placed in operation in many rural areas; and some state library agencies were strengthened by an increase in the size of their staffs.[4]

In 1964, the Library Services Act was amended and renamed the Library Services and Construction Act. This Act extended the 1956 Library Services Act in two important ways: (1) federal grants were made available to urban as well as to rural areas without library services or with inadequate services and (2) federal grants were authorized for the construction of library buildings in those areas lacking the facilities necessary for the development of library services. Although the Library Services and Construction Act will help to extend quality library service to a considerable number of people, much is yet to be done, since in 1961 there were still 18 million rural persons with no convenient access to a public library, and 110 million more with access to libraries that were inadequate according to minimum state standards. In addition, there were 60 million urban residents with inadequate libraries and 1.5 million without public libraries.

It should be kept in mind, moreover, that while the total sum of federal money made available for improvement of public library service was approximately tripled by the 1964 Library Services and Construction Act, this larger sum was for service to a much larger number of people, due to the inclusion of the urban population, and that per capita aid actually decreased from 18 cents to 13 cents.

The Federal government, in addition to strengthening public libraries, provided financial assistance in 1964 which made it possible for libraries to work with state and community organizations in the fight against poverty. This assistance was provided under Title I of the Library Services and Construction Act and the Economic Opportunity Act of 1964. Four of the seven titles of the Economic Opportunity Act made it possible for libraries to serve either as an instituting agency or as a community educational resource center, or both, in combating one of the major problems relating to poverty—lack of education. The funds provided librarians with the opportunity to prove that, in addition to serving the educated community, they could also be effective in assisting the 40 or 50 million Americans who were culturally deprived. Library programs in this area include work with children from low-income families, the aged, young adults, the functional illiterate, and the illiterate. In carrying out these programs, librarians are cooperating with a number of community organizations to help meet the educational and cultural needs of the underprivileged.

Service to Students

The population of the United States, expanding at the rate of 3 million a year, totaled 191 million in 1964. This rapid growth in population has resulted in a marked increase in school enrollments. During the decade ending in 1963, the total population had increased by 18.5 percent, while the number of young people (between the ages of 5 and 19) increased by 40 percent. This latter group, the most frequent users of libraries, increased from 35 million in 1950 to almost 50 million in 1960, and is expected to increase to 60 million by 1970.

In 1964, the higher postwar birth rate had resulted in a major increase in college enrollments. The college-age group (now over 10 million) is expected to increase to 14 million by 1970 and to 16 or 17 million by 1980. It is estimated that there will be almost twice as many students in the nation's colleges by 1970 if college enrollments increase at the same rate as they have since 1960. As spectacular as the population growth has been, it has been paralleled by a tremendous surge in knowledge with the consequent production of more books and journals. Moreover, where once a single textbook was sufficient for a course, educators at various levels now are encouraging individual research and collateral reading, resulting in a much greater use of libraries.

By 1985, the total number of college graduates is expected to increase to 18 million, compared with the 1960 total of 8.1 million. This represents an increase of 122 percent. During the same period the total adult population is expected to increase only 60 percent. The accelerating number of college graduates represents an increase in the public library's potential audience of active readers. In 1957, it was estimated that one third of all public library users were college graduates.

Public libraries have been concerned with the mechanics of how best to serve the constantly expanding number of library users—students and others—and how to cope with the various problems arising from limited facilities. The amount of material needed to answer student questions is often insufficient, and communication among public, school, and college librarians is often lacking. The public librarian attempting to provide adequate service to students must endeavor to gain financial support for an improved book stock, building, and staff or he may find he is curtailing service to adults. Public libraries are thus faced with the serious problem of developing adequate facilities as well as of finding an adequate means of providing service to meet the needs of both students and adults.

Many librarians realize that the increased use of public libraries by students may be expected to result in a substantial improvement in library services. For decades, librarians have dreamed of and worked toward the day when educators would make maximum use of the library. That day has arrived. It is now up to the librarians and the communities which support them to take advantage of the opportunities to expand.

Beginning in the early 1960's, many state library associations had been devoting meetings or entire conferences to the subject of expanding library use, and the professional library press contributing a considerable number of articles on the student use of libraries. In 1963, following a proposal by ALA President James E. Bryan, a three-day meeting —referred to as a "Conference within a Conference"—was held as part of the annual ALA Conference. The official title of the meeting was "An Inquiry into the Needs of Students, Libraries, and the Educational Process."[5] A total of 4,000 librarians from all types of libraries studied the situation and concluded that service to students represented not a problem but rather an opportunity for the library profession.

Following the Conference within a Conference, a study of student use of libraries in one community was undertaken by Lowell Martin. The results of this study appeared in *Students and the Pratt Library: Challenge and Opportunity*.[6] In 1964, expanded National Defense Education Act legislation provided financial assistance for school libraries by establishing summer institutes for improving the qualifications of school librarians and by supplying library materials in certain subject areas.

These various conferences, discussions, research studies, and articles produced recommendations such as the following for librarians and educators:

Find out what is needed by students in a particular community and what is already available

Develop cooperative relations and work together to achieve the common goal of providing effective library service

Define the respective functions of the several kinds of libraries serving students

Establish a working plan to maintain closer contact between the school and the public library

Increase financial support in order to bring all libraries up to the recommended standards

Further a better understanding of the role of reading in secondary education

Maintain longer hours of opening by school libraries

Develop better communication between classroom and library

Secure physical facilities to handle the increasing student load

Promote closer contact between teachers and librarians so that librarians may become more familiar with the school curriculum and teachers more familiar with the materials available for class assignment

Encourage cooperation in materials selection by school and library personnel

Segregation in Public Libraries

Events relating to segregation occurred during the four-year period beginning in 1960. Professional librarians, acting through the American Library Association, brought considerable pressure to bear on the elimination of discriminatory practices in public libraries. Two Virginia public libraries reacted to the 1960 federal desegregation order by closing their doors to all persons, white and Negro.

In 1961, a special ALA Committee on Civil Rights presented an amendment to the Library Bill of Rights at the ALA Midwinter meeting. This amendment, which was passed by the ALA Council, stated: "The rights of an individual to the use of a library should not be denied or abridged because of his race, religion, national origins or political views."

Later that year, the Chairman of the ALA Intellectual Freedom Committee, Archie L. McNeal, presented two recommendations to the ALA annual meeting in Cleveland. The first was that the American Library Association, through its Executive Board, should bar from membership any state library association which practiced discrimination. The second was that foundation funds should be sought for a study of the freedom of access to library materials in all libraries in the United States.

During the latter half of 1961, the Petersburg (Virginia) Public Library reopened as a desegregated library, and the libraries at Greenville, South Carolina, and Memphis, Tennessee, were desegregated. Two states, Texas and Kentucky, made important moves to end library segregation in 1962.

That same year racial tensions increased, and the ALA adopted a new statement on membership. It called upon all members to work for equal access to library resources and to eliminate barriers to professional advancement for librarians because of race or religious belief. Three years were allowed state chapters to show progress in the elimination of discriminatory practices. At the same meeting an announcement was made of grants totaling $35,000 to be used for a research study on free access to public libraries.

The long-awaited *Access to Public Libraries* report was published by the American Library Association in 1963. This report, prepared by International Research Associates, Inc., covered four areas relating to freedom of access: (1) restrictions on race, (2) restrictions on students, (3) limitation on foreign language resources, and (4) regional distribution of library resources.

The ALA Library Administration Division held a series of meetings to evaluate the report, and upheld and commended the findings relating to two areas: (1) segregation as it limited access to libraries and (2) the regional distribution of library resources. The Division concluded that the sections of the report dealing with limitations on foreign language resources and with restrictions on students were not sufficiently developed to be significant.

The most controversial section of the report was the one investigating the possibility of indirect discrimination through location and services of library branches in large northern cities. The Board of Directors of the Library Administration Division stated that "this portion of the survey attempted an excursion into a most complex area of library practice where administrators are still struggling to find the right way in an infinite variety of patterns. This excursion was much too shallow." Further study was recommended.[7]

The major conclusions of the report relating to limitations of access to library services based on race were as follows:

Library desegregation in the 16 southern states had proceeded considerably further than the desegregation of other public facilities, such as schools, swimming pools, and transportation.

Widespread and severe segregation remained in the 5 southern states of Mississippi, Alabama, South Carolina, Louisiana, and Georgia.

Library segregation was far more prevalent in the smaller cities and towns and in the rural areas than in the larger cities of the south.

The rate of library integration had been increased by the widespread belief of professional librarians that it was their duty to provide service equally to all members of the public.[8]

In 1964, the American Library Association continued to study problems of segregation in libraries. At the 1964 ALA Conference in St. Louis, the membership voted that ALA officers and staff members should not attend, in an official capacity, the meetings of any state association which was not able to meet the requirements of chapter status in the American Library Association.

Other Developments

Between 1957 and 1964, other significant factors influenced public library development, such as the rapid growth of mass media, increased library building, research and demonstration relating to the mechanization of library processes, the establishment of National Library Week, and the work of the Small Libraries Project of the American Library Association.

During the past ten years, a major revolution in communications technology has taken place in the United States, highlighted by the successful launching of a communications satellite. The majority of Americans today have easy access to a variety of mass communication media, and much research interest has been centered on the use of these media: who uses them, how much they are used, and why they are used. The findings of such research have implications for the public library and are useful in determining the library's present-day role. Mass media include newspapers, radio, television, magazines, motion pictures, and books—of which there were 28,451 new titles or editions published in 1964. No one medium has established itself as superior for communicating knowledge of all kinds to all audiences.

While most communication agencies have profit as a primary goal, public libraries are concerned with service. Research has shown that the audiences of different media tend to overlap and that an individual rarely is receptive to only one medium. Furthermore, it has been found that exposure to various media on the part of an individual is more effective in providing him with information than exposure to only one. The role of the public library is not to compete with commercial agencies of mass media, but rather to provide the services that these agencies are not equipped to give. Some librarians have concluded that the public library should put major emphasis on its educational and cultural functions and less on its recreational function, because the commercial agencies of mass media are better equipped to perform this function.

Between 1957 and 1964, cities and towns in the United States increased in size, numerous suburbs came into being, and a considerable number of new public library buildings, with informal exteriors and attractively decorated interiors, were designed. Bond issues were voted for the erection of buildings, and library systems were established to serve new areas. This growth and expansion have continued unabatedly.

An independent, nonprofit corporation, the Council on Library Resources, Inc., was established in September, 1956, to assist in improving the resources and services of libraries, and to aid in solving the problems of libraries generally and research libraries in particular. The Council received an initial grant of $5 million in 1956 from the Ford Foundation, and a second grant of $8 million from the same source in 1961. The primary interests of the Council are: (1) basic research in the processes of distribution, organization, storage, and communication of knowledge and (2) methodological development toward improvements of technique and improvements effected through coordination of effort as the result of cooperation and standardization.

During the late 1950's, Joseph L. Wheeler, former librarian at Enoch Pratt Free Library, proposed a national effort to help small libraries, and suggested a series of publications directed toward community librarians and trustees. The Small Libraries Project, supported by a grant from the Council on Library Resources, was designed to provide reliable information about the organization, operation, and administration of the small public library.

In 1958, the National Book Committee and the Junior Chamber of Commerce joined librarians in sponsoring the first National Library Week, which was held during the week of March 16–22. Newspapers, magazines, and radio and television stations stressed the importance of libraries in American life. In 1961, the ALA Committee on Evaluation of National Library Week reported an increase in book circulation, in financial support, in cooperation with community organizations and the involvement of community resources and personnel in the library's program, and in public interest in libraries as a result of the week's promotion. National Library Week is now established as an annual event.

Two major library exhibits gave millions of people a glimpse into the library of the future. They were the Library 21 exhibit, which opened at the Seattle World's Fair in 1962, and the Library/USA exhibit which opened at the New York World's Fair in 1964. The information center at the Library 21 exhibit featured an electronic computer which compiled bibliographies and made available, by mechanical retrieval, the opinions of ancient philosophers. A learning resources center at the same exhibit displayed library uses for closed-circuit television, tapes, films, illustrations, copying machines, and devices for instant communication. The Library/USA exhibit in New York featured an electronic ready reference service; a computer and communication system demonstrating the impact of technology on the library; a modern children's library; and an adult reading and browsing area. All of the Library/USA information services were planned around the subjects exhibited in the huge Federal Building and supported the Federal theme of "Challenge to Greatness."

Role of the American Library Association in Library Adult Education

Adult Services Division

In 1957, the American Library Association established the Adult Education Division at its Midwinter meeting. Later that year, at the annual conference, the Association changed the name to the Adult Services Division and appointed Eleanor Phinney as the executive secretary of the Division.

The Division was assigned responsibility for ALA's activities in the area of library service designed to further continuing educational, cultural, and recreational development of the adult population. This responsibility broadened that of the former Adult Education Section of the Public Libraries Division, which stressed the adult education function. Adult services was broadly defined to include indirect guidance services, reader guidance services, services to organizations, library-sponsored group programs, and services to the community.

Under the leadership of its officers and executive secretary, the program of the Division is carried out through the investigation of various areas of adult services in all types of libraries by divisional committees, implementation of special projects, preparation of publications, presentation of programs at the annual ALA Conference, publication of two divisional newsletters, and cooperation with national organizations and federal agencies. The activities of the Division have helped to develop a better understanding of the ways in which libraries can serve individuals, groups, and various segments of the adult population, such as community groups, labor groups, the aged, and illiterates. To implement adult services, the Division provided information on techniques used in various areas, such as television, reading improvement, film utilization, reading guidance. The Division increased knowledge concerning the use of community resources in providing more effective service to adults, provided reading guides in various subject areas, prepared materials to facilitate the programs of national organizations and federal agencies, identified materials for use in study-discussion programs, and worked on standards for adult services.

The activities of the Division are too diversified to be described here, but some of the major ones may be singled out for brief mention. Eleanor Phinney's surveys of library service to the aging, made in 1957 and 1958,[9] helped to stimulate additional interest in this area of library service. In 1959, the Institute on Library Service to an Aging Population was held during the ALA Conference. In 1960, a survey of state library activities in the field of aging was carried out by the Adult Services Division Committee on Library Service to an Aging Population. This survey provided valuable basic information for the 1961 White House Conference on Aging.[10] In 1961, the Division cooperated with the White House Conference on Aging and, in 1964, prepared and issued a statement of the "Library's Responsibility to the Aging."

Since its inception, the Division has had a continuous program of publications. In 1958, the ASD Committee on Bibliography of Library Adult Education produced guides on program planning, book talks, and television. The following year a guide to the literature on reading habits and interests of adults was made available. By 1963, ten guides had been prepared and distributed by the Division. Other major publications of the Division include: *Guide for Developing a Public Library Service to Labor Groups,* issued in 1958, and *Adult Services: A Handbook for State and Regional Library Associations,* published in 1961.

The "Reading for an Age of Change" project, which was initiated by the Division, was established in 1960 with a grant from the Carnegie Corporation of New York. This project, developed along the lines of the "Reading with a Purpose" series, was designed to serve the mature and intelligent library reader. The first Carnegie grant was for five guides, with future guides to be published if response to these original five was adequate. Titles for the first five guides were: *Space Science, The Contemporary Arts, Freedom of the Mind, Expanding Population in a Shrinking World,* and *The World of Economics.* Each contained an introductory essay by a recognized authority and an annotated list of books for further reading. Additional titles are now in process.

The first three reading guides—*Space Science, The Contemporary Arts,* and *Freedom of the Mind*—were introduced at the 1962 ALA Conference. Suggestions about ways to make effective use of the reading guides were presented, and plans for evaluating the series of guides were developed. The Carnegie Corporation approved the application for renewal of the supporting grant in 1963. Five new subjects for guides were chosen. These were cultural anthropology, philosophy, political science, contemporary poetry and drama, and biology. Two new guides, *Man and His Government* and *Contemporary Drama,* were begun in 1964.

The Division has played an active role in cooperating with national groups and organizations. In 1960, it participated in the preparation of reading lists, an ALA exhibit, and kits of materials for use as background material for the White House Conference on Children and Youth. The Division also prepared a set of guidelines for library cooperation, and later adapted it for use in cooperating with planning for the White House Conference on Aging in 1961. An ALA exhibit and kits of materials again were supplied for the White House Conference on Aging, and four issues of a newsletter were circulated, designed to provide stimulation and information for libraries planning activities in connection with the Conference. In 1961, the Division helped to stimulate interest in the American Assembly's discussion program on the report to the President's Commission on National Goals, "Goals for Americans." This was done by preparing a set of guidelines to outline the methods and steps to be taken, distributing a list of materials, and encouraging community-wide discussion.

One of the major strengths of the Adult Services Division has been the ability of its members to identify and anticipate major societal needs, such as the problems of the aged and the culturally deprived. Several years in advance of the "Poverty Program," the Division explored ways of assisting the illiterate and functionally illiterate.

The May, 1963, ASD Newsletter included a guide to library adult education, entitled "Adult Reading Improvement," containing a bibliography and discussion of reading improvement as a field of library service. The next month a one-day preconference Institute on Reading Improvement for Adults was held at the annual ALA Conference, and a standing committee on that subject was formed. The guide and the preconference Institute were based on the results of a survey of programs of reading improvement in public libraries in towns of more than 15,000 population. In 1964, a $7,000 grant was made to the Adult Services Division for a preliminary field study on methods and materials for public library service to functionally illiterate adults.

Between 1957 and 1964, the Adult Services Division helped to develop a better understanding of the way in which the educational objective was related to the activities and services in all types of libraries; encouraged study and experimentation in developing new and better methods of working with individuals and groups; and provided a sound foundation for the future development of the field of adult services.

Library-Community Project

On September 1, 1955, a grant of $200,000 from the Fund for Adult Education made it possible for the Office of Adult Education of the American Library Association to establish the Library-Community Project. Two years later an additional grant of $200,000 from the same source made it possible to extend the project to August 31, 1960.

The Library-Community Project assisted libraries to plan long-term adult education programs based on an analysis of community needs. It developed and broadened the work and experience of previous ALA adult education projects supported by the Fund for Adult Education, which included the American Heritage Project, the Survey of Adult

Education in Public Libraries, the Adult Education Subgrant Project, and the Allerton Park Conference on Training Needs for Librarians Doing Adult Education.

The Library-Community Project was organized into three program areas. The first was the continuation, on a limited scale, of the American Heritage Project in the grant areas that were in their first or second year of operation. The second was the provision of consultant service in adult education on a national basis, and the third was the development of long-term adult education programs in selected states based on an analysis of community needs.

Eight libraries were selected for pilot study. They were the Ottawa (Kansas) Public Library, the Clinch-Powell (Tennessee) Regional Library, the Hackley Public Library (Muskegon, Michigan), the Hastings (Nebraska) Public Library, the Shawano (Wisconsin) City-County Library, the Ardmore (Oklahoma) Public Libraries, the Cumberland County (North Carolina) Library, and the Wicomico (Maryland) County Library. In addition to the 8 grant states which contained the pilot library projects, 23 states received consultant service, and 30 states —participating in regional or state library associations—received program or staff assistance. More than 5,000 librarians, trustees, and lay people participated in 89 major activities designed to develop library interest, knowledge, and skills.

The success of the eight pilot libraries in studying their communities, and later developing adult education programs, was determined by three factors: (1) the readiness of the libraries to undertake the study, (2) the leadership available within the individual libraries and on their boards of trustees, and (3) the unpredictable elements.

The fact that the pilot libraries were making a contribution to the profession of librarianship was emphasized throughout all phases of the Project, and emphasis was placed on the fact that failure was as important as success. The Project was judged not on the achievements of the library and the community, but on the body of knowledge that the activities yielded for other libraries. Participating agencies and individuals were gratified by the desirable new directions taken by the pilot libraries following completion of the Project.[11] The pilot libraries made a genuine contribution to librarianship. Their work led to the development of the process described in *Studying the Community: A Basis for Planning Library Adult Education Services*.[12] The overall contribution of the Library-Community Project, in the opinion of the writer, was not what occurred during the period of the Project but what came about as a result of this Project: (1) more knowledge about the process of studying the community; (2) more sensitivity to the ways in which the library could develop services to help meet community needs; and (3) more awareness of the library's role as an active educational agency of the community. The influence of both the Library-Community Project and the Adult Services Division is reflected in the major literature on adult educational services written during this period.

Literature of Adult Services

Library adult education has gained considerable impetus from the increase of theoretical and practical knowledge reflected in the literature of adult services since 1956. Since that time, the quality and the quantity of the literature have shown a marked increase. This is particularly true in the areas of community study, service to the aged, and descriptions of specific types of adult services. In addition, there has been a growth in the literature on the philosophy and history of library adult education, adult needs and interests, societal changes which have implications for services, and reader guidance.

The following titles represent some of the major contributions to the literature of library adult education since 1956:

1956

National Society for the Study of Education. Committee on Adult Reading. *Adult Reading,* ed. by Nelson B. Henry. Chicago: The Society; distributed by the Univ. of Chicago Pr., 1956.

Phinney, Eleanor. *Library Adult Education in Action: Five Case Studies.* Chicago: American Library Association, 1956.

1957

Houle, Cyril O. "Strengthening the Influence of the Public Library," *ALA Bulletin,* 51:765–71 (Nov. 1957).

Lacy, Dan M. "The Adult in a Changing Society: Implications for the Public Library," *Library Quarterly,* 27:279–93 (Oct. 1957).

Powell, John Walker. "Join the Community—Risk or Opportunity?" *ALA Bulletin,* 51:363–65 (May 1957).

1958

American Library Association. Adult Services Division. ASD Guide to the Literature of Libraries and—

No.1	Program Planning	June, 1958
No.2	Program Planning, Supplement	May, 1961
No.3	Television	June, 1958
No.4	Reading Interests and Habits of Adults, 1942–1958	June, 1959
No.5	Service to the Aging	June, 1959
No.6	Film Utilization	June, 1960
No.7	Service to Labor	June, 1960
No.8	Reading Guidance	July, 1960

No.9   Services to Community Agencies and
            Organizations   June, 1961
No.10   Reading Improvement for Adults   July, 1963
Chicago: The Association. Adult Services Division, 1958–1963. (mimeographed)

1959

Gregory, Ruth W. "Adult Education Services in Public Libraries—1959," *ALA Bulletin*, 53:787–91 (Oct. 1959).

Stone, C. Walter, issue ed. "Current Trends in Adult Education," *Library Trends*, July 1959.

1960

American Library Association. Library-Community Project Headquarters Staff. *Studying the Community: A Basis for Planning Library Adult Education Services*. Chicago: The Association, 1960.

Stevenson, Grace T. "Adult Education in Libraries," in *Handbook of Adult Education in the United States*. Chicago: Adult Education Association of the U.S.A., 1960.

1961

Ulveling, Ralph A. "Lose Not Our Greatest Strength," *Mountain Plains Library Quarterly*, 6:5–9 (Winter, 1961).

Wessells, Helen E. *The Public Library for Lifelong Learning*. Washington, D.C.: U.S. Office of Education. Library Services Branch, 1961.

1962

Gregory, Ruth W. *Library Service for Adults*. (No.10, Small Libraries Project) Chicago: American Library Association, 1962.

Lyman, Helen H. *Reader's Guidance Service in a Small Public Library*. (No.8, Small Libraries Project) Chicago: American Library Association, 1962.

Phinney, Eleanor. *A Study of Current Practices in Public Library Service to an Aging Population: An Evaluative Report*. ("Occasional Papers," No.62) Univ. of Illinois Graduate Library School, Nov. 1961.

1963

Librarianship and Adult Education: A Symposium, ed. by Antje B. Lemke. Syracuse, N.Y.: Syracuse Univ. School of Library Science, 1963.

Monroe, Margaret Ellen. *Library Adult Education: The Biography of an Idea*. New York: Scarecrow, 1963.

Phinney, Eleanor. "Recent Trends in Public Library Adult Services," *ALA Bulletin*, 57:262–66 (March 1963).

Public Library Service to Adults. Madison, Wis.: Wisconsin Free Library Commission, 1963.

Stevenson, Grace T. "Library Adult Education Activities in Public Libraries of Germany, Denmark, and England," *ALA Bulletin,* 57:643–54 (July–Aug. 1963).

1964

Stevenson, Grace T. "Recent Developments in the Methods by Which People Are Encouraged To Use Public Libraries and Improve Their Personal Interests through Books in the United States of America," *Libri,* 13, no.3–4:285–96 (1964).

Educational Objective and Role of the Public Library

A change in the interpretation of the public library's educational objective occurred during the late 1950's, when more emphasis was placed on the need for continuing education for adults, stressing the idea that the formal education received ten or twenty years ago was now inadequate in a rapidly changing world. Also, with the organization of the ALA Adult Services Division, the concept of library adult education was broadened. In 1962, Eleanor Phinney, Executive Secretary of the Adult Services Division, stated that the term adult services "does not indicate a shift away from adult education. On the contrary, it is based on the concept of the library as an educational institution, and signifies that the educational objective is built into all of the library's activities and services."[13]

The educational role of the library during the late 1950's and early 1960's was based on the philosophy of integrating the library with the community it served. It involved a thorough knowledge of the importance as well as of the educational benefits of working with community groups and organizations; of understanding the objectives, interests, and activities of community groups; of participating in the planning of community activities; and of helping the library to become a more active force in the community. The gradual acceptance of this role was due to a number of factors. The major influences were the philosophy of community service stressed in *Public Library Service,* the community approach to library adult education which was emphasized in all the activities of the Library-Community Project, and the continuous program of publications, activities, and conferences of the Adult Services Division.

Educational Services

During this same period educational services for adults were directed toward community development, civic enlightenment, personal development, and social improvement, with major emphasis on community development.

Trends

A survey of adult educational services in a selected group of libraries was made by the ALA Office for Adult Education in March, 1959. Ruth Gregory, in commenting on the findings of this survey, stated that the "one subject field to which libraries of all sizes gave major attention (with the acquisition of materials, assignment of staff responsibility, and active programming) was Community Development."[14] Programs of community development, said Miss Gregory, "have been realistically geared to local situations and have resulted in community action and a spread of public confidence in the library as a participant in constructive community studies and action programs."[15] Another major concern of librarians during the period from 1959 to 1964 was the attempt to provide service to the "difficult to reach" groups in society: the aged, labor, illiterates, and the culturally deprived. In the implementation of educational services to adults, there was a marked trend toward focusing services on community needs and problems, cooperating with community groups and organizations, cosponsoring activities with other community agencies, and utilizing community talent.

The approach in providing services for adults showed a noticeable change during the late 1950's. In contrast to the traditional types of services provided by libraries during the late 1940's and early 1950's, librarians during the period from 1957 to 1964 were more individualistic in respect to the development of services. Ruth Gregory, in her analysis of the 1959 ALA adult education survey, said:

> The survey indicates that library adult education as practiced in all parts of the country is moulded by self-discovered local needs. . . .
> . . . .
> that the library of 1959, regardless of size, has adopted all of the modern techniques for the promotion of adult education services and backs them up with the acquisition of printed materials in quantities needed by the program.[16]

A 1959 U.S. Office of Education publication[17] provided data on adults participating in educational activities. The results, based on a 1957 Current Population Survey, showed that 7.8 percent of the adults in the United States were estimated to have participated in adult education classes at some time during the preceding year; of the participants in adult education, 95 percent were white and 5 percent nonwhite; the West had the highest rate of adult education participation with 1 participant to every 7 nonparticipants; and two thirds of the persons participating in adult education lived in urban areas.

In 1962, Eleanor Phinney, Executive Secretary of the Adult Services Division, conducted a survey to obtain information and opinions on trends in public library service to individuals and groups, through a

questionnaire addressed to state library extension agencies. The major
findings of this survey indicated that there was a trend from:

A leaning toward recreational reading to recognition of the importance of reference and informational services

Dependence on a limited staff to the involvement of more people in
the library's program

Striving as individual libraries to meet standards of good library
service to cooperation between libraries in the state in a variety
of ways to accomplish their objectives

Library service within the library, only, to service throughout the
community

Emphasis on service to children to emphasis on service to all ages

Use of books alone to use of all media of communication

Satisfaction with service to individuals, only, to awareness of the fact
that the individual's needs may be expressed either alone or within
a group, and that groups have corporate interests over and above
individual interests[18]

From 1955 to 1964, the library literature recorded an impressive
list of educational services to adults. Of the articles devoted to educational services, there were 59 articles on service to the aging and 59
on discussion groups. On reader guidance, 29 articles appeared during
the period, and service-to-labor articles numbered 27. There were 20
articles on film forums and 17 on book talks. Program planning was
the subject of 16 articles, and service to hospitals was the topic of 7.

Service to the Aged

During the late 1950's and early 1960's, more emphasis was placed on
public library services to the aged. The growing population of older
citizens and the problems they faced inspired many book-related adult
educational programs throughout the libraries of the country. These
programs served as a source of information on various aspects of the
aging process and helped to make the public aware that such information
was available. Another part of the service program was to consider
the needs of the aging person as an individual and to provide the materials that would best meet his needs. Public libraries served senior
citizens who were institutionalized by providing collections of books.
They also provided ceiling projectors to be used by bedridden patients
in reading, and large-print books for those with failing eyesight.

The libraries also stimulated group programs to serve the aged. The
1961 Winter edition of *Maryland Libraries*[19] published an article suggesting that librarians plan programs of appeal to older persons, but
not for them exclusively, and use older persons in planning such programs. The article also suggested that librarians should consider their

work as an information service, to direct older citizens to agencies that could be of assistance to them.

In 1961, the University of Illinois Library School published an article by Eleanor Phinney[20] in which were noted the activities provided by libraries to meet the needs of older people, listed in the order of frequency. The most common activity was that of providing books, followed by publicizing materials for the aged. Next, were the provision of shut-in service, work with other agencies to help the aged, providing a meeting place, and providing films and similar materials. The same article contained a table listing the topics used in programs and activities designed to bring information on aging to the general public. The top four topics were: Use of Leisure Time, Preparation for Retirement, Family Relations, and Mental Health.

Individual library programs designed for the aged included the weekly noon-hour, winter season book reviews of the Grand Rapids (Michigan) Public Library and of the Gary (Indiana) Senior Citizens Library Club. The 1960-61 Annual Report of the District of Columbia Public Library described the "Going Like Sixty" Club meetings held in its branch libraries.

The West Georgia Regional Library established an Armchair Travelers Club. The Seattle Public Library had a creative writing class for people over sixty. The Cleveland Public Library program for the aged included an Annual Institute on Education in Later Years, which was cosponsored by the library, the *Cleveland Press,* and the Cleveland Welfare Federation. The Public Library of Charlotte and Mecklenburg County in North Carolina held a workshop which resulted in the establishment of a permanent Committee on Aging. These are but a few examples of the programs developed by public libraries for the senior citizen in this period.

In 1964, the Adult Services Division adopted a statement on the library's responsibility to the aging. It reads as follows:

Aging is a life-long attribute of man which consequently has daily, personal implications for each person in our society. The social, economic, and biologic problems resulting from the process of aging place a responsibility on every school, public and academic library, and every special library having a general education function, as well as those libraries with a specific concern for the problems and needs of the aging and the aged.

These libraries serve their communities by—

1. contributing to a positive, wholesome attitude toward aging and the aged

2. providing information and education on the subject and its problems
   for the professional and the layman who work with this group,
   for those who are aging, and for those who are retired

3. demonstrating by example in the library profession and in the

use of volunteers the potential contribution to society of the retired
or the eligible to retire

4. facilitating the use of library service to the aged
5. providing library service appropriate to the special needs of this group
6. working with other institutions and groups concerned with these
   problems and needs
7. continually exploring ways of making these services more effective.

   Such service should respect the existing philosophy of library service,
should use the traditional library materials and services, should
maintain adequate standards, and unless the library is a specialized
library serving the aging or aged, should serve the aging and aged as a
part of integrated adult services.

Materials

During the early 1960's, there was an increase in the circulation of
nonfiction and of audio-visual materials, especially recordings. The
decline in the use of the library for leisure-time reading and the increase
in the use of the library for serious reading were due largely to the
growing popularity of television, greater participation by the public
in group activities and spectator sports, the availability of a larger
variety of recreational activities, and the growth of the paperback in-
dustry and book clubs. These developments provided adults with a
wider range of recreational activities which, in many instances, absorbed
some of the leisure time formerly spent in reading light fiction provided
by the public library. At the same time, the improvement of nonfiction
collections in many public libraries and a growing national emphasis
on the values of education encouraged the trend toward serious reading.

Stimulation

Efforts were made to stimulate library patrons to make greater and
more effective use of library materials. The following examples of how
book lists and book reviews have increased library use point up the
growing effort of public libraries to help keep the community aware
of current problems, needs, and issues; to call attention to these concerns; and to encourage further reading.

In 1960, the Newark (New Jersey) Public Library issued a revised
edition of its book list, "How Do Your Children Grow?" to schools and
service agencies. Requests were received from 24 schools and agencies
for 12 to 300 copies each, and a total of 5,500 copies was distributed.
In the same year, the New Haven (Connecticut) Free Public Library
distributed 3,000 copies of a book list on the presidential election. A
collection of 110 adult titles, considered to be the best books, grew
from 543 volumes to 844 volumes because new titles were added weekly
when all copies of a given title were checked out.

During the past nine years, many public libraries have expanded their book-reviewing programs and thus further stimulated interest in reading and the use of libraries. In the year April, 1961–March, 1962, the staff of the St. Louis Public Library gave 1,181 book reviews. The following year the St. Louis staff filled 1,326 requests for book reviews.

Advisory Services to Individuals and Groups

Along with book reviews and book list distribution, many public libraries established or expanded their advisory service to individuals and groups. Three examples of this increased interest in advisory service may be noted: at the Cincinnati Public Library, the Akron (Ohio) Public Library, and the Pittsburgh Public Library. At Cincinnati, in 1959, a supervised home study program at the Library served more than 200 individuals who came regularly for assistance. In Akron, the Library's Group Service Department helped plan 435 programs for other organizations in 1959. In Pittsburgh, the Public Library developed an outstanding program of advisory services.

Library-sponsored Discussion Groups

One of the most popular of the group services provided by public libraries since 1957 has been the library-sponsored discussion group. In 1957, the Great Decisions program was part of the group service programs of public libraries in Michigan—particularly in Detroit and Kalamazoo—in Oregon, and in Indiana. In the Cuyahoga County Public Library System in Ohio, one branch had two monthly world affairs discussion groups, and other groups used a newspaper feature called "Spotlight Topics" to stimulate youth discussion groups.

The Decatur (Illinois) Public Library conducted a discussion group entitled "Main Street Forum," which took its discussion topics from the front pages of newspapers. In Santa Barbara, California, the Public Library sponsored a four-meeting program on Pasternak's Nobel Prize-winning novel, *Dr. Zhivago*. The series received wide and favorable comment throughout the city.

In Miami, Florida, discussion group programs of the Public Library were all initiated by request. The programs began with a workshop to explore techniques by which any topic, no matter how controversial, could be discussed intelligently and objectively. Subjects chosen for discussion included: The Handicapped—Aides and Friends; Unions and the Right-To-Work Law; Castro's Revolution; Our Secret Weapon—Thinking; and What Is the Individual's Responsibility to Society?

The Akron (Ohio) Public Library, in 1959, sponsored or cosponsored 109 meetings on Great Books, the Civil War, and other topics. The Indianapolis Public Library, during 1960–1961, had an average attendance of 67 people at each of 25 Thursday-evening programs at its central library. It sponsored 24 adult Great Books groups, 2 young adult groups, and 2 junior groups. In Cincinnati, the Public Library sponsored 31 Great Books groups, including 4 for high school students. These are but a few of the examples of library-sponsored discussion groups which formed an important part of the libraries' educational services to adults during this period.

Special Programs

During the past eight years, special programs have become an increasingly important part of the educational services of public libraries. These programs utilize a variety of approaches and cover a wide range of areas, from reading improvement to music, drama, history, poetry, lectures, forums, and films.

The reading improvement programs are aimed at helping library patrons read faster and with better comprehension. The Brooklyn Public Library began a reading improvement program in 1953, and in 1961 reported that it had served more than 1,500 persons from 18 to 35 years of age. At that time, the program had a waiting list of from 200 to 600 persons. The course continued through 1964, and the Library, in cooperation with Brooklyn College, conducted a study to determine the effect on the 1,197 people who had completed the 24-hour course. The conclusion was that motivated students would make significant gains in reading comprehension and speed, regardless of the mechanical aids used, training, instructor, or other factors. The 1,197 students had 2,275 readers' advisory interviews.

In 1960, almost 18,000 people attended film showings at the Enoch Pratt Free Library in Baltimore. The films were shown both at the central library and in the branch libraries. In Indianapolis, attendance at a 1960 special program entitled "An Investor's Forum" ranged from 150 to 200 participants at 5 weekly meetings. The program was sponsored by the Business Department of the Indianapolis Public Library.

In 1960, the first of six Sunday lectures drew 1,400 people to hear Alistair Cooke speak at the Enoch Pratt Free Library. The Library reported the same year that 800 people were present at a book and author luncheon, and 2,500 people attended 31 noon-hour lectures, of which 15 were on foreign affairs. In 1961, the Racine (Wisconsin) Public Library sponsored 5 lectures attended by 2,620 people. During the year 1962–1963, the Brooklyn Public Library sponsored 509 adult programs, including chamber music concerts, a course on the history of the Negro, and dramatic presentations, with a total of 14,488 people (averaging 27 persons per program) attending the programs during the year.

During the period from 1957 to 1964, then, there was more emphasis on the development of special programs in cooperation with community groups and agencies, more acceptance of service to groups, and more time given to the development of specific types of services to particular groups in the community. Many of the group services and special programs considered to be innovations during the 1930's and 1940's were generally accepted by librarians in 1964. As Ruth Gregory has said, "Libraries are more than willing to explore a local situation, to experiment with new ideas and techniques, to initiate and to cooperate, and to give and to take in the process of fulfilling a goal of purposeful service to individual adults and to groups."[21]

Looking to the Future

Although much has been accomplished by the public library in the field of adult education, new vistas of service are appearing. Some contemporary developments which may be expected to create new and different demands on libraries for service are:

Rapidly expanding, highly mobile population

Increasing number of United States citizens over 65, many of whom have low incomes

High rate of high school dropouts

Growing problems of urbanization

Increase in leisure time

Steady rise in the educational level of the population, especially among the 20- to 35-year-old age group

Rate at which automation is eliminating jobs, affecting youth without experience, older workers, men and women in depressed rural and urban areas, and members of minority groups

These and other factors, such as the problems of the functional illiterate, present a major challenge to the public library, which is directly involved in providing materials and services to the persons affected by these problems and in working with other community organizations and agencies in assisting them. Much still remains to be done.

Summary
and Conclusions

The purpose of this study has been to describe the evolution of the adult educational commitment of the American public library, with particular attention to the most prevalent interpretations of the library's educational objective and the most common educational services provided in each period discussed. This concluding chapter will review the discussion of the evolution of the educational commitment and services of the American public library; present the major phases in the development of the public library as an educational institution; discuss a number of factors which affected the formulation and implementation of the library's educational objective; present some suggestions for improving the library's educational responsibility; predict future trends in public library development; and recommend areas for further research relating to the educational commitment and services of public libraries.

Review of the Study
Educational Objective of the Public Library

The American public library was established during the middle of the last century to serve adults who could read and who had the incentive to do so. The educational objective of this new institution was to provide adults, and particularly those who had received a common or elementary school education at public expense, with the means to continue their education through reading and private study. This aim was based on the belief that the work of the public schools would be ineffective if no means were available for the working adult to continue his education.

During the last quarter of the nineteenth century, the conception of the public library as an institution for continuing education was broadened. The librarians of this period believed that a public library existed because education should not stop when an individual stopped going to school, because formal schooling was but the first stage of education, and because the better part of every man's education was that which he gave himself. Self-education through libraries was described as a process in which an individual obtained ideas and information independently from books, and was characterized as a form of education for which the individual alone was responsible and over which no authority or teacher presided. With the further elaboration of both the assumptions and the process of self-education, librarians interpreted the library's educational objective as the provision of a means by which adults, and particularly those forced to leave school to earn a living, could continue their education through their own efforts, at their own rate, and to the extent of their own abilities.

As a result of the widespread development of elementary school education and the steady growth of the secondary school in this country between 1890 and 1910, librarians, during the first two decades of this century, adjusted their educational objective to changing conditions and attempted to provide adults—particularly those who were unable either to attend high school or to complete it—with the means to continue their education.

With the rapid increase in the educational level of the adult population between 1920 and 1964, librarians of this period gave less attention than their predecessors had to the remedial aspects of the library's educational work. The educational objective gradually changed from emphasis on helping adults to make up for their lack of formal schooling to encouraging all adults to use their leisure creatively and to increase their understanding. Thus, from the early 1930's to 1964, the library's educational objective was not focused on any particular group of adults; instead, the aim was to provide all adults with the means to educate themselves continuously.

The educational objective of the public library can be divided into two parts: what is intended and for whom. On the basis of this classification, the "what is intended" part was to provide the means of self-education. This part of the objective remained substantially unchanged throughout the period from 1850 to 1964. The "for whom" part of the library's educational objective did change, however, as a result of the gradual rise in the educational level of the adult population.

Educational Role

The educational role of the public library, between 1850 and 1885, was to serve as a supplement to the public school system: "to continue and increase the effects of that system by the self-culture that results from reading." Then, between 1885 and 1915, library leaders, seeking a more substantial role for the library, began to assert that the library's educational role was not to supplement but to complement the work of the public schools. It was suggested that the public school and the public library were two parts of one complete purpose, and that each of these institutions was inadequate without the other. Librarians were urged by leaders of the profession to help create among the general population a conception of the public library as a "people's university," a community institution whose educational role was to take up the education of citizens at the point where it was discontinued by the public schools.

With the rapid growth of adult educational agencies and programs between 1920 and 1956, the library's educational role gradually shifted from serving as an integral part of the community's system of public education to participating and cooperating with other adult educational institutions and agencies. The educational role during the late 1950's and early 1960's was based on the philosophy of integrating the library with the community it served: cooperating with community groups, participating in the planning of community activities, cosponsoring educational programs with other community agencies, and providing the library's own programs based on community needs and interests.

Educational Goals

The most common educational services provided by public libraries between 1850 and 1964 were directed toward five specific educational goals. Two of these goals, civic enlightenment and personal development, remained constant throughout this period. Moral betterment was a goal from around 1850 to 1890, vocational improvement a major goal during the years between 1930 and 1950, and community development of major concern from 1957 to 1964.

Educational Services

The number and type of educational services provided by the majority of public libraries changed in a gradual and additive fashion between 1850 and 1964 from (1) the provision of materials to (2) the provision of materials and personal assistance to (3) the provision of materials, personal assistance, and stimulation to (4) the provision of materials, personal assistance, stimulation, and service to groups. During the early years of library development (1850–1875), the collection of library books was a primary concern. The librarians of this period performed their educational function by supplying a collection of books of educational value. These books were provided, without charge, for use by the adults of the community. Initiative concerning their use, however, was left entirely to the library user, who was allowed to consult books only within the walls of the library building.

As library collections increased in size, librarians turned their attention to the development of systematic procedures for classifying and organizing library resources. In order to make books more accessible inside the library, librarians pioneered, during the last quarter of the nineteenth century, in devising methods for arranging and locating books on the shelves. In attempting to remove some of the barriers which in the past had made libraries uninviting to the public, librarians adopted new operational policies—such as the circulation of books for home reading, open access to shelves, and longer hours of opening—and provided personal assistance to readers in locating and selecting books.

Between the turn of the century and the beginning of World War I, librarians, seeking ways to encourage readers to visit the library frequently, took steps to reduce inconvenience and difficulty in obtaining library books. They helped to make library resources accessible close to the homes of readers by establishing substations and branches and by organizing traveling and county libraries. Also, in attempting to attract a larger clientele, librarians began to publicize the library's services. The adoption of this aggressive philosophy of library service had its effect on the library's educational work. In addition to providing materials and personal assistance, librarians began to devise methods to stimulate adults to read material of educational value. This was done by preparing and distributing book lists, setting up book displays, and giving book talks to community organizations. The creation of motivation, which began during this period, later became a much more elaborate and extensive practice of public libraries.

Between 1920 and 1956, the majority of public libraries in this country did not go beyond the provision of materials, personal assistance, and stimulation in carrying out their educational function. However, a number of the large and some of the medium-sized libraries did go beyond this point. They provided guidance for the individual reader during the 1920's and 1930's, and sponsored informal educational programs for adult groups during the 1940's and 1950's.

The major characteristic of library development between the close of World War I and the beginning of World War II has been aptly termed "the emergence of the reader." It was a period when various types of research were undertaken to find out more about the reading interests and habits of adults. As a corollary to the emphasis on the individual reader, some libraries provided readers' advisory service, which consisted of planning personalized reading programs and selecting books in accordance with the individual's reading ability. Reader guidance was a unique educational service that other distributors of books could not provide, and it was the first conscious attempt by librarians to direct a systematic learning process.

Following the close of World War II, some libraries began to emphasize the provision of educational services and programs for adult groups. These services consisted of calling attention to the programs and courses of the adult educational agencies of the community and supplying printed materials. The major type of library-sponsored group programs, such as varied book and audio-visual programs, discussion and forum programs, and program planning institutes, were designed to promote effective educational use of library materials.

Between 1957 and 1964, the concept of library adult education was broadened in an attempt to build the adult educational aim into all the library's services and activities. In providing educational services for adults, a trend began toward developing library services based on community needs and interests, cooperating with all types of community agencies, cosponsoring activities, and utilizing a variety of techniques in providing the library's own program. The major change during the period was the gradual acceptance by librarians of services and programs for groups.

Development of the Public Library as an Educational Institution

Four major phases in the development of the public library as an educational institution may be noted:

First Phase

Almost a century and a half of experimentation in the development of three types of semipublic libraries in this country—parish, social, and circulating libraries—prepared the way for the establishment of the first public library, which was organized in Peterborough, New Hampshire, in 1833. The effective beginning of the American public library movement, however, came in 1854, when a public library was established in Boston by a small group of learned and influential citizens.

The Boston Public Library was organized for the purpose of providing a means by which adults could continue to learn through their own efforts. This purpose was based on three beliefs. First, adults were capable of unlimited self-improvement and intellectual progress. Second, books were the principal instrument of education. Third, most adults could not afford to buy the books they needed to continue their education through reading. These beliefs, which were clearly formulated and concisely recorded by the founders of the Boston Public Library, provided a rationale for the establishment of public libraries in this country from around 1855 to 1875.

During this early period of public library development, librarians had a clear understanding of the library's educational aim and of the way in which it was to be implemented. They believed that it was not their responsibility to teach or to instruct the library patron, but instead to provide him with the type of books from which he could gain for himself the knowledge he wanted. In working with a relatively small and homogeneous audience, librarians provided a specific type of educational service which they rendered with as little intrusion as possible into the lives of the persons they were serving.

Second Phase

During the last quarter of the nineteenth century, the public library gradually expanded its services and acquired two additional objectives: recreation and reference. Librarians believed that the provision of recreational reading (namely, popular novels) would lead to more serious reading, contribute to cultural growth, and thereby serve as a stepping-stone to the library's primary objective—education. They reasoned that they must first interest the reader before they could educate him; and, to this end, "must commence at his own standard of intelligence." During the late 1870's and throughout the 1880's, the library's educational objective was basic, however, and the other two objectives were subordinated to it. Then, around 1890, when the provision of recreational reading and informational reference service began to make more and more demands on the librarian's time, confusion arose about which of the library's three objectives—education, recreation, or reference—was primary. In serving an audience composed of persons with diverse reading interests and abilities, librarians had difficulty in making an absolute division between the educational objective and the recreational objective. Furthermore, they were faced with the problem of determining how much time and how many resources should be devoted to each.

With the rapid growth of the public library movement after 1900, librarians directed major efforts toward serving a larger and more heterogeneous audience, responding to more of the recreational reading wants of the people, and increasing library coverage and circulation. The majority of librarians were no longer seriously concerned about whether novel reading led to serious reading. This attitude was fostered and sanctioned to some extent by the development, during the early 1900's, of the organized recreational movement in the United States, which began with the recognition of the fact that the urban environment offered no adequate outlet for the wholesome energies of either children or adults. Recreation was "socially useful," and therefore it was "good" public policy for libraries to supply recreational reading which would help people pass time pleasantly. Thus the recreational objective soon exceeded the educational objective in terms of emphasis.

Third Phase

Following the close of World War I, a small group of librarians attempted to revitalize the library's educational objective and to make education once more the dominant function of the public library. This group sought a return to the educational ideals of the founders, attempting to bring those ideals to fruition through a new interpretation adapted to the needs of the 1920's. During this period more public libraries began to function successfully as adult educational agencies. Many of the advances that came about during the 1920's can be attributed to the work of the American Library Association, which, with funds from the Carnegie Corporation of New York, provided encouragement and assistance to libraries in the development of educational services for adults. Although some positive gains resulted from these efforts, the concept of the library's educational commitment was not clearly understood by the majority of librarians.

With the coming of the depression of the 1930's, library appropriations were reduced. Subsequently, there was a reappraisal of essential library services, and some of the leaders of the profession stated that the educational rather than the recreational services of libraries would be more likely to command public respect, especially during the period of financial crisis. Between 1933 and 1938, two attempts were made to formulate comprehensive statements of public library objectives. Each of these statements, which were officially adopted by the American Library Association, represented a step forward in focusing attention on the library's educational responsibility.

A series of events which occurred between the close of World War II and 1956 resulted in a gradual improvement in the quality, and an increase in the quantity, of educational services for adults through libraries. Two additional attempts were made to formulate comprehensive statements of public library objectives, and in each of these statements the educational function was given first place among the listing of objectives. During this period, two survey studies of library adult education were undertaken which presented the first detailed account of the extent and diversity of the adult educational services to groups provided by public libraries. Several extensive projects were initiated by the American Library Association, with financial assistance from the Fund for Adult Education, which increased the number and type of the adult educational services of libraries. The results of these efforts were that more librarians were gradually acquiring a better understanding of the library's educational responsibility and more libraries were beginning to allocate staff time and resources to the provision of adult educational services and programs.

Fourth Phase

Between 1957 and 1964, increased emphasis was placed on the provision of reference and informational services, less emphasis was given to the provision of materials for recreational or pastime reading, and the concept of educational service to adults was broadened by building the educational aim into many of the library's services and activities and by focusing services on community needs. Reference and informational service increased because of the greater use of the public library by students. The need for providing recreational reading, especially light fiction, decreased because of more diversified recreational outlets for adults—such as television, spectator sports, group activities—and the availability of inexpensive paperbound books for recreational reading. Educational services for adults through the public library were focused more and more on local community concerns, were often planned and cosponsored by the library and another agency, were presented by means of a variety of techniques, and were often more meaningful to adults than the more traditional type of programs presented by libraries during the late 1940's.

Thus, there have been four phases in the development of the public library as an educational institution. First, the library began as a single-purpose institution in which education for adults was the central aim. Next, it became a multipurpose institution in which education, recreation, and reference were the primary objectives, with recreation and reference eventually taking precedence over education. Third, it entered a period of appraisal in which attempts were made to revitalize its educational objective. Fourth, it is currently placing major emphasis on its informational and educational objectives and less on its recreational objective.

Factors Hindering the Implementation of the Adult Educational Objective, 1890–1950

Although the library's educational service to adults was the earliest and one of the most fundamental of the library's objectives, it was, during the period from around 1890 to 1950, often the most misunderstood as well as the most neglected. In the opinion of the writer, three major factors hindered the effective implementation of the library's adult educational aim during this period.

First, there was the historical conflict between the provision of educational services and the provision of recreational services. In attempting to maintain and augment library budgets, some librarians tried, between 1890 and 1950, to increase book circulation by showing an extreme readiness to obey any clearly expressed demand of the public for recreational reading. As a result, these librarians had difficulty in allocating adequate resources and staff time to educational services for adults. Such services usually did not contribute substantially to increasing circulation, and increased circulation (like increased sales) was often the standard measure by which success of a public library was judged.

Second, the controversial nature of library adult education discouraged some librarians, during the period from 1924 to 1950, from engaging actively in the provision of educational services for adults. The controversy, which continued for almost thirty years, was the result of conflicting opinions concerning the proper meaning of library adult education, the appropriate role of the library in community adult education, and the means to be used in providing educational services.

Third, no adequate statement was available concerning the nature of the library's adult educational objective during the period from 1924 to 1956. Hence this objective—to facilitate informal self-education of all people in the community—was not intelligible or specific enough to serve as a guide in planning educational services, or to provide a major unifying force for the public library. Between 1938 and 1958, the attempt to define or describe the library's adult educational aim and function was discouraged by some librarians because they maintained that such an attempt would inhibit innovation and creativity and tend to standardize educational services for adults. Needless to say, this point of view was not shared by all librarians.[1]

Lacking the direction afforded by a clear philosophy, suffering frequently from an emphasis on means without a proper consideration of ends, and being guided at times not by rational thinking but by enthusiasm, library adult education was not—despite the many positive gains made in this area between 1924 and 1956—accepted by the majority of librarians as a legitimate library function. Between 1957 and 1964, the concept of library adult education was broadened, and there was greater acceptance among librarians concerning the provision of diversified educational service to adults. Some of this change can be attributed to the work of the ALA Adult Services Division and the ALA Library-Community Project.

Although considerable progress has been made in recent years in extending the scope and diversity of educational service to adults, there is, in the opinion of the writer, a need for further refinement of the meaning of library adult education—a need to explore and discuss not only the "how" but also the "why" and the "what" of such education.

Suggestions for Improving
the Library's Educational Responsibility

The following propositions, or *suggestions,* deal with the nature of the public library's adult educational objective and the aspects of library service provided to realize this objective. The intent is not to present a rigid formula, or even a broad philosophy of the library's adult educational work, but rather to discuss some of the essential elements of the library's adult educational aim and function. This may, in turn, *suggest* some guidelines by which progress may be achieved toward a more adequate statement of the library's educational responsibility to adults.

Educational Process

Education is a process by which an individual, either through his own efforts or with the assistance of another individual or a group, purposely develops abilities, acquires desirable attitudes, and gains new knowledge. This process consists of purposeful learning, which is different from random and incidental learning experiences.

The educational process, within the library context, is concerned with intellectual, vocational, cultural, aesthetic, personal, and community development. It does not consist exclusively of fact finding and the pursuit of incidental information, and its primary concern is not relaxation, amusement, escape, or therapy.

Educational Aim

The educational aim or objective of the public library is concerned with those educational ends which the library considers to be desirable and which it wishes to achieve. In planning educational services, it properly distinguishes between the long-run objective that it hopes to achieve and the short-run goals that help it to move toward the objective. The long-run educational aim is focused on furthering continuing education and may be manifest in specific goals or particular ends-in-view,[2] such as increasing self-realization and personal awareness; improving the social and economic environment; extending civic enlightenment; or emphasizing the role of community awareness, informed opinion, and rational intelligence in the area of collective and personal decisions and actions. Once the long-run aim is clarified, specific, short-run goals are determined, and appropriate steps are undertaken in order to achieve one or more of these goals.

Educational Function

The educational function is concerned with those library services and activities that are undertaken in order to achieve the desired educational aim. Educational services, which are means, should not be confused with the ends to be achieved or considered as ends in themselves. Without a clear end-in-view, the library does not perform its educational function merely by deciding that it might be a good idea to organize a library-sponsored discussion group, to emphasize particular types of library materials (films, recordings, and the like), to call attention to specific problems or issues, or to provide some special service for a particular segment of the adult population (parents, migrants, young adults, or the aged).

The library's adult educational function is performed by providing appropriate means for adults to continue to learn, but only when there is a purposeful aim pursued within the context of librarianship. It is directed toward a specific end and is implemented by providing services designed to stimulate further learning. This function, however, is not performed by all libraries in the same way. Differences exist among communities in terms of adult needs and interests, and differences among libraries in terms of staff skills and library resources to help meet these needs. Usually, no library will perform its educational function effectively unless the chief librarian has a clear and sympathetic understanding of the library's educational responsibility to adults.

Performing the Educational Function

Although the term "education" has the connotation of schooling and formal instruction, the performance of the library's educational function does not involve transforming the library into a public evening college or changing the librarian into a classroom teacher. The educational aim of the public library, however, should be the same as that of institutions of formal instruction—to educate. Only the means of implementation should be different.

The major function of schools and colleges is to teach, while the educational function of the public library is performed by providing materials, assistance, stimulation, group services, and special services or programs. The librarian helps to facilitate self-education by such means as providing materials of educational value for those persons who wish to continue their education through reading and private study; supplying assistance for those persons who seek guidance in their reading; providing informal learning opportunities (discussion groups, film forums, and so on) for those persons who seek the stimulation of other adults in continuing their education; and motivating the non-learner, through displays, book lists, and book talks, to continue his education. The librarian is a helper, adviser, and stimulator, and the person seeking further learning through the use of the library is constantly made to feel responsible for his own education.

The public library, in implementing its educational function, does not infringe upon the responsibility of any other community institution or agency whose primary function is educational. The public library and the institutions of formal education complement each other in their educational work; the virtue of each is that it is not the other. The educational work of the public library should be developed along library lines; any attempt to imitate or emulate the practices of formal education will impair the effectiveness of the library's educational services.

Educational Services

Educational services for adults are basic to the central purpose of the public library; they are not extra or special services. Although educational service is fundamental, it should not be provided to the detriment or neglect of other library services. The library's educational services are provided for the purpose of contributing to the voluntary educational development of the individual; they are not forced or imposed upon him by the librarian. The patron makes his own decisions—the librarian, however, may give assistance, if requested, to help the patron make his decision—as to the way in which he will continue his education through the use of library resources and services, and he proceeds at his own rate and to the extent of his own abilities.

Designing Educational Services for Adults

In contrast to formal education, where the student is required to adjust to the traditional subject divisions of the academic curriculum, informal education for mature men and women is based on their interests and aspirations; is directed toward the achievement of goals which they feel to be real and significant; and is concerned with the use of methods suited to their needs and characteristics.

The most important educational task of the librarian is materials selection. The core or basis of *all* the library's educational services—regardless of what form they may take—is a collection of library materials of educational value, especially books, which deal with current issues, perennial problems, and the areas, roles, and stages of human life about which adults wish to have more knowledge. This does not mean, however, that educational service is synonymous with the circulation of nonfiction. The educational responsibility of the librarian is to promote purposeful reading of worthwhile books, either fiction or nonfiction. Effective educational service can be provided to the fiction reader as well as to the reader who prefers to learn through the use of current and authoritative nonfiction.

Clientele for Educational Services

The men and women *most* likely to seek opportunities for continuing education are those who have attended institutions of higher education and who have some aim in their learning. Although relatively little research has been done on the motives for education during adulthood,[3] it is clear that the more formal education a person has, the more likely he is to seek opportunities for continued learning, and that different people become aware of their need for further education at different periods of adult life.

The continuing learner cannot be described precisely. A very general and incomplete portrait of him might depict him as a young, socially adjusted, and well-educated person, between the ages of twenty-eight and fifty, who wishes to keep his mind fresh and alive, to make his experiences vivid and meaningful, and to utilize his talents fully and effectively. In brief, he wants to improve himself; this is his realistic and primary aim in his continuing learning activities.

Those persons interested in continuing their education into adult life are still a small, though rapidly growing, minority of the population. Less than half of all adults in this country participate in any form of continuing learning during their lifetime. More specifically, it is esti-mated[4] that one out of every five adult Americans (or 25 million adults) participated in some form of adult education during 1962. From the library's point of view, it is significant that over one third (or approxi-mately 9 million) of these persons were engaged in independent self-instruction, while the other two thirds utilized other methods, such as attending classes, lectures, and talks; participating in group discussion; taking courses via correspondence and educational television; being exposed to on-the-job training; or seeking instruction from a private teacher.

What is the library's responsibility toward those adults who wish to continue to learn through their own efforts? The report of the Public Library Inquiry of 1950 recommended that the library's primary func-tion should be to serve that group of adults "whose interest, will, and ability" lead them to seek personal enrichment and enlightenment. Although the library may seek to enlarge this "natural library audience," the evidence of the Inquiry report substantiates the conclusion that the process of enlargement is slow, "requiring intensive efforts and not producing numerically spectacular results." The major efforts of public libraries, according to the Inquiry report, should be directed toward providing adequate informational and educational services to this small but select group of natural library users. If this were done, it was sug-gested, a social contribution would result much greater than might be indicated by the gross numbers involved.[5]

Individuals interested in continuing their education are faced with obstacles. These difficulties are stated not in order to discourage library efforts but that the potential audience for the library's educational ser-vices may be considered in proper perspective. The fact that time and energy for education for adults are in short supply should be taken into account. Furthermore, the mature individual, in addition to dealing with the pressures and problems of daily life, must be willing to submit himself to the discipline required to increase his knowledge and under-standing. Perseverance and a willingness to use effectively one's leisure time are essential. This does not mean that adult learning is an unpleas-ant, grim, or boring activity. The contrary is nearer the truth; the personal satisfactions to be derived from intellectual activity are, for some persons, superior to the satisfactions derived from any other form of endeavor. Enjoyment and learning are not antipathetic. Effective learning, however, does require time and effort.

Evaluating Educational Services

The educational services of the public library should not be evaluated entirely in terms of increased circulation, increased number of registered borrowers, or—as is frequently suggested—in "relation to the promotion of reading." Many values are derived from reading, but the librarian's efforts to promote *all* types of reading, although desirable, are not necessarily educational. What is read, the purpose for which it is read, and the degree of active participation in what is being read are distinguishing factors. Reading is an important part of learning but only under certain conditions. People who read a considerable number of books each year are not necessarily those who are most effectively continuing their education. Reading can become a compulsion, an indulgence, or an escape. A person may read continuously and learn nothing; he may read in a passive way without exercising his mind or his emotions in any way.

The major criterion of the library's educational services is whether the librarian's efforts have been effective in facilitating self-education. To evaluate the library's educational services, however, involves certain difficulties. Attempts can be made to devise means to evaluate the efficacy of the services, but so long as the belief exists that this type of service deals entirely in intangibles, no evaluative progress can be made. Circulation figures, as is well known, do not supply the necessary distinctions and are not entirely an effective measure of the library's worth. Librarians, however, cannot continue to assume that libraries are always educationally "good" and therefore deserve public support. Intuitive judgments may be easy to defend, but they contribute little toward increasing the value of the library as an educational institution.

Specific methods for evaluating the library's educational services cannot be outlined in detail here, but a few general principles may be suggested. First, the objective of a particular type of educational service should be clear, specific, and realistic. If it is not, little or no progress can be made toward determining the extent to which the objective is achieved. Second, the objective should be operational in that it should indicate the nature of the desired outcome, that is, whether the outcome is directed toward gaining new knowledge or understanding, acquiring desirable attitudes, or developing skills and abilities. Third, the method of evaluation to be used (interview, observation, questionnaire, attitude survey, or the like) should be appropriate to the change in knowledge, attitudes, or skills that is being assessed. Fourth, the time and effort spent in evaluating services should be in accord with the value of the information sought.

Next Phase of Public Library Development

It is the opinion of the writer that, as a result of the work initiated under the Library Services Act of 1956, adequate public library service will be available by 1975 to the entire population. By 1980, the average library expenditure per capita will be doubled. Library collections will increase in terms of both size and quality. Larger units of library service will be established. Education and reference will become primary objectives, and recreation will eventually become a very minor concern. Books will continue to be the basic means of implementing library objectives, but the use of other media will increase substantially. Library procedures will become more efficient, and advances will be made in library technology that will result in freeing librarians from some of the routine phases of library work.

The educational level of the population of the United States will be raised, and a high degree of literacy attained. More book titles will become available in paperbound form, and more copies of paperbound books will be sold. Many pronouncements will be given about the cultural revolution in America, but the reading of serious books will not become a mass activity.

The public library will serve an increasing number of the adult population. This audience will be composed primarily of persons who are well-educated and interested in ideas and serious reading. In serving this audience, the public library of the future will become, in the final analysis, as effective an educational institution as librarians are willing to make it.

Recommendations for Further Research

Further research relating to the educational commitment and services of the public library is needed if the library is to fulfill adequately its role in the future. A few suggestions for such research follow. First, in the implementation of the educational services of public libraries, there is a need for reliable knowledge about which library materials and services possess most educational value for various groups of adults; the characteristics of books that influence public opinion and change the attitudes of readers of average intelligence and education; and how knowledge transmitted through library materials is absorbed and utilized by adults who wish to continue to learn through their own efforts.

Second, there is a need for evidence about the educational value of various types of library services and programs to serve as a reliable guide in the planning and development of such programs and services. Third, the educational work of the public library is based, for the most part, upon unexamined assumptions. There is a need for analytical study of the ideas upon which the provision of educational services and programs of public libraries is based.

This study has identified and described the way in which several generations of public librarians have recast the fundamental conception of the educational aim of the public library during their own time and set of changing circumstances. It has indicated some of the reasons why the present educational ends and practices of public libraries were adopted. The intent has been not only to provide a historical account of the educational commitment and services of public libraries but also to develop an initial study which might be useful for more detailed investigations of this subject by others.

Notes

Chapter I
Collecting and Preserving Books, 1833–1875

1. Arthur Alphonse Ekrich, Jr., *The Idea of Progress in America: 1815–1860* (New York: Columbia Univ. Pr., 1944), *passim*.
2. Before 1830, the book was practically the only mediator of learning, the only distributor of serious thought.
3. Albert Smith, *History of the Town of Peterborough, Hillsborough County, New Hampshire* (Boston: George H. Ellis, 1876), p.114–17.
4. Bernard C. Steiner, "Rev. Thomas Bray and His American Libraries," *American Historical Review,* 2:59–75 (Oct. 1896); William D. Houlette, "Parish Libraries and the Work of Rev. Thomas Bray," *Library Quarterly,* 4:588–609 (Oct. 1934); Charles K. Bolton, *Proprietary and Subscription Libraries* (Chicago: ALA Publishing Board, 1917); William I. Fletcher, "The Proprietary Library in Relation to the Public Library Movement," *Library Journal,* 31:C268–72 (Aug. 1906); Sidney Ditzion, "Mechanics' and Mercantile Libraries," *Library Quarterly,* 10:192–219 (April 1940); Charles K. Bolton, "Circulating Libraries in Boston, 1765–1865," Colonial Society of Massachusetts, *Publications,* 11:196–207 (Feb. 1907).
5. Jesse H. Shera, *Foundations of the Public Library* (Chicago: Univ. of Chicago Pr., 1949), p.181–99.
6. Justin Winsor, "M. Vattemare and the Public Library System," *Literary World,* 10:185 (June 7, 1879).
7. Josiah P. Quincy, "The Character and Services of Alexandre Vattemare," *Massachusetts Historical Society Proceedings,* 1, 2d ser.: 260–72 (1884).
8. Winsor, *op cit.,* p.186.
9. Horace G. Wadlin, *The Public Library of the City of Boston: A History* (Boston: Printed at the Library and published by the Trustees, 1911), p.8, 9.
10. Edward Edwards, *Free Town Libraries: Their Formation, Management, and History, in Britain, France, Germany, and America* (London: Trubner and Co., 1869), p.281.

11. The complete text of the New Hampshire Act of 1849 is reprinted in Shera, *op. cit.*, p.192–93.
12. (Jared M. Heard), *Origin of the Free Public Library System of Massachusetts* (Clinton, Mass.: Printed at the office of the *Saturday Courant,* 1860), p.9.
13. Paul Revere Frothingham, *Edward Everett, Orator and Statesman* (Boston: Houghton, 1925), p.323.
14. "A Public Library," *Massachusetts Teacher,* 4, no.8:255–56 (Aug. 1851).
15. George Ticknor, *Life, Letters and Journals of George Ticknor* (Boston: James R. Osgood and Co., 1876), 2:301.
16. *Ibid.*
17. *Ibid.*, p.301–2.
18. *Ibid.*, p.304.
19. Wadlin, *op. cit.*, p.31.
20. *Ibid.*, Ticknor, *op. cit.*, p.305; Shera, *op. cit.*, p.181.
21. Shera, *op. cit.*, p.181.
22. *Report of the Trustees of the Public Library of the City of Boston,* City Document No. 37, July 1852, p.6.
23. *Ibid.*, p.6–9.
24. *Ibid.*, p.15.
25. *Ibid.*, p.8.
26. *Ibid.*, p.20.
27. *Ibid.*, p.21.
28. Wadlin, *op.cit.*, p.41–42.
29. Edward Edwards, *Memoirs of Libraries: Including a Handbook of Library Economy* (London: Trubner and Co., 1859), 2:215.
30. A different interpretation has been suggested by Jesse H. Shera: "The public library, as we know it today, came about through the effort of small and highly literate groups of professional men—scholars, lawyers, ministers, and educators—who sorely needed books for the performance of their daily tasks and who, through their efforts, convinced their respective communities of the social utility of supporting a public library. Even George Ticknor, who, more emphatically than most, argued for the public library as an agency of popular culture, helped fill the shelves of the new Boston Public Library with titles that more properly belonged in the study of the man of letters" ("On the Value of Library History," *Library Quarterly,* 22:246 [July 1952]). Shera's point of view, in the judgment of the writer, is relevant with regard to the early *practices* of public libraries but not with respect to the *motives* of the founders. Shera's interpretation assumes that the founders of the Boston Public Library established a tax-supported municipal library primarily for the purpose of advancing their own personal interests, and, to achieve this end, set about to convince the people of the social value of a public library. The evidence that Shera gives to support this interpretation is that Ticknor "helped fill the shelves of the new Boston Public Library" with scholarly books. The fact is that Ticknor donated some books (not "filled the shelves") from his personal collection. Since almost all public libraries were, and still are, receptive to donations of significant books, and because it was never stated, implied, or assumed that the book collection of the Boston Public Library would consist entirely of popular books, the example that Shera cites as evidence of the motives of the founders is questionable. Moreover, Everett and Ticknor, the two central figures in the establishment of the Boston Public Library, were not "sorely" in need of "books for the performance of their daily tasks." Both men had their own

private collection of books, as well as access to the Boston Athenaeum and the Harvard College library. Furthermore, Everett, who served as Secretary of State from November, 1852, to May, 1854, the period in which the Boston Public Library was being established, also had access to the Library of Congress. Ticknor, according to Arthur E. Bestor, Jr., had a private library consisting of "some thirteen thousand volumes" ("Transformation of American Scholarship, 1875–1917," in Pierce Butler, ed., *Librarians, Scholars and Booksellers at Mid-Century: Papers Presented before the Sixteenth Annual Conference of the Graduate Library School of the University of Chicago* [Chicago: Univ. of Chicago Pr., 1953], p.10).

31. Merle Curti, *The Social Ideas of American Educators, with a New Chapter on the Last Twenty-Five Years* (Paterson, N.J.: Littlefield, Adams, 1959), p.51–100.

32. During the early years of public library development, library books were to be used only by adults. Library service to children did not begin in most libraries until after 1900. See Arthur E. Bostwick's *The American Public Library* (New York: D. Appleton, 1929), p.81–99.

33. Leon Carnovsky, "The Public Library in the U.S.," *Libri,* 2:287 (June 1953); William S. Learned, *The American Public Library and the Diffusion of Knowledge* (New York: Harcourt, 1924), p.68; Sidney Ditzion, *Arsenals of a Democratic Culture* (Chicago: American Library Association, 1947), p.174; Ernestine Rose, *The Public Library in American Life* (New York: Columbia Univ. Pr., 1954), p.217.

34. U.S. Bureau of Education, *Public Libraries in the United States of America: Their History, Condition, and Management* (Washington, D.C.: Govt. Print. Off., 1876), p.452–56.

35. *Ibid.,* p.762–72.

36. *Ibid.,* p.1012–42.

37. Bartholomeus Landheer, *Social Functions of Libraries* (New York: Scarecrow, 1957), p.167.

38. *Report of the Trustees of the Public Library of the City of Boston,* City Document No.89, 1875, p.17.

39. Arthur E. Bostwick, ed., *The Library and Society: Reprints of Papers and Addresses* (New York: Wilson, 1920), p.91.

40. There were, however, exceptions to this policy. The lending of library books was permitted in some small libraries. Among the large libraries the Boston Public Library, during its early years of operation, would lend a book if a deposit were made on it. Later, library policies were relaxed. In 1879, Ainsworth Spofford wrote, "Of all the great collections, it [the Boston Public Library] is the only one which lends out books free of charge to all citizens." See his "The Public Libraries of the United States," *Journal of Social Science,* 2:108–9 (1879).

41. Melvil Dewey, "Field and Future of Travelling Libraries," *Home Education Bulletin* (University of the State of New York, No. 40), Sept. 1901, p.6.

Chapter II

Organizing Resources, 1876–1897

1. Samuel Swett Green, *The Public Library Movement in the United States: 1853–1893* (Boston: Boston Book Co., 1913), p.18.

2. George B. Utley, *Fifty Years of the American Library Association* (Chicago: American Library Association, 1926), p.11.

3. Green, *op. cit.* [Justin Winsor, William Frederick Poole, Frederick Morgan Crunden], p.25–34, 210–11; William Parker Cutter, *Charles Ammi Cutter* (Chicago: American Library Association, 1931); Robert Kendall Shaw, *Samuel Swett Green* (Chicago: American Library Association, 1926); Chalmers Hadley, *John Cotton Dana* (Chicago: American Library Association, 1943); Linda A. Eastman, *Portrait of a Librarian: William Howard Brett* (Chicago: American Library Association, 1940).

4. Josiah P. Quincy, "Free Libraries," in U.S. Bureau of Education, *Public Libraries in the United States of America: Their History, Condition, and Management* (Washington, D.C.: Govt. Print. Off., 1876), p.390.

5. Melvil Dewey, "The Profession," *Library Journal*, 1:6 (Sept. 1876).

6. Charles Francis Adams, Jr., "The Public Library and the Public Schools," *Library Journal*, 1:437 (Aug. 1877).

7. William E. Foster, "The School and the Library: Their Mutual Relations," *Library Journal*, 4:319 (Sept. 1879).

8. Moses Coit Tyler, "The Historic Evolution of the Free Public Library in America, and Its True Function in the Community," *Library Journal*, 9:47 (March 1884).

9. James Russell Lowell, "Books and the Public Library [1885]," in Arthur E. Bostwick, ed., *The Library and Society* (New York: Wilson, 1920), p.90–91.

10. Frederic B. Perkins, "Public Libraries and the Public, with Special Reference to the San Francisco Free Public Library," *Library Journal*, 10:228 (Sept.–Oct. 1885).

11. James M. Hubbard, "Are Public Libraries Public Blessings?," *North American Review*, 149:340 (Sept. 1889).

12. Samuel Swett Green, "Address of the President," *Library Journal*, 16:3 (Dec. 1891).

13. Josephus N. Larned, "Address of the President," *Library Journal*, 19:4 (Nov. 1894).

14. Henry M. Utley, "Address of the President," *Library Journal*, 20:4 (Dec. 1895).

15. "American Library Association: An Editorial," *Library Journal*, 3:43–44 (March 1878).

16. U.S. Bureau of Education, *Public Libraries in the United States of America: Their History, Condition, and Management* (Washington, D.C.: Govt. Print. Off., 1876), p.xi.

17. Henry M. Utley, *op. cit.*, p.3.

18. Dewey, *loc. cit.*

19. U.S. Bureau of Education, *loc. cit.*

20. William Howard Brett, "Address of the President," *Library Journal*, 22:4 (Oct. 1897).

21. Melvil Dewey, "Librarianship as a Profession for College-bred Women," *Library Notes*, 1:43 (June 1886).

22. U.S. Bureau of Education, *loc. cit.*

23. Melvil Dewey, "Libraries as Related to the Educational Work of the States," *Library Notes*, 3:333 (Sept. 1888).

24. *Ibid.*, p.335; the spelling of words is that used by Dewey.

25. Lowell, *op. cit.*, p.91.

26. Adams, *op. cit.*, p.436.

27. Quincy, *op. cit.*, p.400.

28. Foster, *loc. cit.*

29. Adams, *op. cit.*, p.437.

30. Josephus N. Larned, "The Mission and Missionaries of the Book," *First Bi-*

ennial Report of the State Library Commission of Wisconsin: 1895–1896
(Madison, Wis.: Democratic Printing Co., 1896), p.28–29.

31. Quincy, *loc. cit.*
32. Foster, *loc. cit.*
33. Dewey, "Libraries as Related to the Educational Work of the States," *Library Notes*, 3:336 (Sept. 1888).
34. William F. Poole, "The Organization and Management of Public Libraries," in U.S. Bureau of Education, *Public Libraries in the United States of America: Their History, Condition, and Management* (Washington, D.C.: Govt. Print. Off., 1876), p.479; Bradford K. Pierce, "The Probable Intellectual and Moral Outcome of the Rapid Increase of Public Libraries," *Library Journal*, 10:235 (Sept. 1885); Joseph Leroy Harrison, "The Public Library Movement in the United States," *New England Magazine*, 10:772 (Aug. 1894); H. H. Barber, "The Free Public Library," *Lend a Hand*, 14:371–72 (Jan.–June 1895).
35. William I. Fletcher, "Public Libraries in Manufacturing Communities," in U.S. Bureau of Education, *Public Libraries in the United States of America: Their History, Condition, and Management* (Washington, D.C.: Govt. Print. Off., 1876), p.408–10.
36. Samuel Swett Green, "Personal Relations between Librarians and Readers," *Library Journal*, 1:74–81 (Oct. 1876).
37. *Ibid.,* p.81.
38. Samuel Swett Green, *The Public Library Movement in the United States: 1853–1893* (Boston: Boston Book Co., 1913), p.305.
39. Pierce, *loc. cit.*
40. Frederick M. Crunden, "Report on Aids and Guides," *Library Journal*, 11:310 (Sept. 1886).
41. Charles A. Cutter, "Common Sense in Libraries," *Library Journal*, 14:C1–8 (Sept. 1889).
42. Lewis H. Steiner, "Future of the Free Public Library," *Library Journal*, 15:C45 (Dec. 1890).
43. Brett, *op. cit.,* p.C3–4.
44. The authors excluded by the majority of libraries were: Horatio Alger, Mrs. Southworth, Mrs. Henry Wood, Mayne Reid, and Oliver Optic (ALA Cooperation Committee, "Report on Exclusion," *Library Journal*, 7:28–29 [Feb. 1882]).
45. "The Proceedings," *Library Journal*, 1:99 (Nov. 30, 1876).
46. William F. Poole, "Some Popular Objections to Public Libraries," *Library Journal*, 1:49 (Nov. 30, 1876).
47. Fletcher, *op. cit.,* p.410.
48. William E. Foster, "Methods of Securing the Interest of a Community," *Library Journal*, 5:245 (Sept.–Oct. 1880).
49. Sidney Ditzion, *Arsenals of a Democratic Culture* (Chicago: American Library Association, 1947), p.183.
50. Charles Francis Adams, Jr., "Fiction in Public Libraries and Educational Catalogues," *Library Journal*, 4:331 (Sept. 1879).
51. William Kite, "Fiction in Public Libraries," *Library Journal*, 1:277–79 (April 1877).
52. Quincy, *op. cit.,* p.393.
53. James M. Hubbard, "How To Use a Library," *Library Journal*, 9:26 (Feb. 1884).
54. Quincy, *loc. cit.*

55. Justin Winsor, "President's Address," *Library Journal,* 6:64 (April 1881); Cutter, *loc. cit.;* Pierce, *loc. cit.*

56. Frank P. Hill, "Fiction in Libraries," *Library Journal,* 15:325 (Nov. 1890).

57. "Reference Work in Libraries," *Library Journal,* 16:297–300 (Oct. 1891); Samuel S. Green, "Libraries as Bureaus of Information," *Library Journal,* 21:324–26 (Sept. 1896).

58. Herbert Putnam, "President's Address," *Library Journal,* 23:C7 (Aug. 1898).

59. John William Wallace, "An Address of Welcome," *Library Journal,* 1:92 (Nov. 1876).

60. Arthur E. Bostwick, ed., *Popular Libraries of the World* (Chicago: American Library Association, 1933), p.287.

61. "Discussion on Access to Shelves," *Library Journal,* 13:309–10 (Sept.–Oct. 1888); Bernard C. Steiner and Samuel H. Ranck, "Report on Access to Shelves," *Library Journal,* 19:87–96 (Sept. 1894).

62. William I. Fletcher, *Public Libraries in America* (Boston: Roberts Bros., 1894), p.140.

63. Albert Predeek, *A History of Libraries in Great Britain and North America,* trans. by Lawrence S. Thompson (Chicago: American Library Association, 1947), p.107.

64. Justin Winsor, "Free Libraries and Readers," *Library Journal,* 1:64–65 (Sept. 1876).

65. William Howard Brett, "Address of the President," *Library Journal,* 22:3 (Oct. 1897).

Chapter III
Extending Services, 1898–1919

1. James H. Canfield, "Library's Part in Education," *Public Libraries,* 14:120 (April 1909).

2. The first state library agency was organized in Massachusetts in 1890; by 1910, thirty-five states had established library agencies for the purposes of encouraging library development, promoting the efficiency of libraries already established, and maintaining a system of traveling libraries (Clara F. Baldwin, comp., *League of Library Commissions Handbook* [Chicago: League of Library Commissions, 1910], p.5).

3. William B. Shaw, "The Traveling Library—A Boon for American County Readers," *American Monthly Review of Reviews,* 17:165–70 (Feb. 1898).

4. Mary L. Titcomb, "A County Library," *ALA Bulletin,* 3:150–52 (Sept. 1909).

5. "Brief Sketch of the Development of County Libraries in the United States," *News Notes of California Libraries,* 3:123–26 (April 1908); Harriet C. Long, *County Library Service* (Chicago: American Library Association, 1925), p.15–45.

6. Josephine A. Rathbone, "The Modern Library Movement," *Public Libraries,* 13:199 (June 1908).

7. Edward A. Birge, "Books and Life," *Library Journal,* 31:205–6 (May 1906).

8. Henry M. Utley, "Library Development in the Past 20 Years," *Public Libraries,* 16:206 (May 1911).

9. Durand R. Miller, comp., *Carnegie Grants for Library Buildings: 1890–1917* (New York: Carnegie Corp., 1943), p.8.

10. Carnegie recalled: "It is, no doubt, possible that my own experience may have led me to value a free library beyond all other forms of beneficence. When I was a working boy in Pittsburgh, Colonel Anderson, of Allegheny— a name I can never speak without feelings of devotional gratitude—opened

his little library of four hundred books to boys. Every Saturday afternoon he was in attendance at his home to exchange books, and it was when reveling in the treasures which he opened to us that I resolved, if ever wealth came to me, that it should be used to establish free libraries, that other poor boys might receive opportunities similar to those for which we were indebted to that noble man" (Theodore W. Koch, *A Book of Carnegie Libraries* [New York: Wilson, 1917], p.8).

11. Quoted in William S. Learned, *The American Public Library and the Diffusion of Knowledge* (New York: Harcourt, 1924), p.70.

12. Burton J. Hendrick, *The Life of Andrew Carnegie* (New York: Doubleday, Doran, 1932), 2:198.

13. Miller, *op. cit.,* p.3.

14. Hendrick, *op. cit.,* p.203.

15. *Ibid.*

16. "That our libraries are buying much of the 'ephemera' of the day," said Herbert Putnam, "is true; are they, however, spending an excessive proportion of their funds in the acquisition of it? And is the tendency to spend more rather than less? Granting both—the fact and the tendency—what of the alternative? Shall they ignore wholly the predominant interest of the public in the literature which is 'current'?" ("Per Contra," *Library Journal*, 40:472 [July 1915]); Pard B. Wright, "How Far Should the Demand of the Public for Popular Books Be Supplied," *Public Libraries*, 13:122–23 (April 1908); "Predominance of Fiction in Public Libraries," *Library Journal*, 30:70–72 (Aug. 1905).

17. In 1901, Charles A. Cutter said: "The librarian will buy the novels of the Miss Jane Porter of today for the ten thousand, and the poems of the Shelley of today—if he can find him—for the one. He will buy the 'David Harums' and the 'Richard Carvels' for the first class and, shall we say, provisionally, the Stephen Phillips, the Rostands, for the other" ("Should Libraries Buy Only the Best Books or the Best Books That People Will Read," *Library Journal,* 26:71 [July 1901]).

18. Edmund L. Pearson, "Evil That Books Do," *Public Libraries,* 16:190–91 (May 1911).

19. Edward A. Birge, "Library Extension," *Public Libraries,* 10:259 (June 1905).

20. John Shaw Billings, "The Public Library: Its Uses to the Municipality," *Library Journal,* 28:293–94 (June 1903).

21. Arthur H. Chamberlain, "Increasing the Efficiency of the Library as an Educational Factor," *ALA Bulletin,* 5:155 (July 1911).

22. Herbert Putnam, "Library Development in the Past 20 Years," *Public Libraries,* 16:203–4 (May 1911).

23. ——— "The Relation of Free Public Libraries to the Community," *North American Review,* 499:663–64 (June 1898).

24. Cutter, *op. cit.,* p.70.

25. H. J. de Vleeschauwer, "Encyclopedia of Library History," *Mousaion,* 2:94 (1955).

26. Mary Eileen Ahern and others, "Reference Work with the General Public," *Public Libraries,* 9:55–65 (Feb. 1904); Linda M. Clatworthy, "Reference Work," *Library Journal,* 31:C263–65 (Aug. 1906); Clement W. Andrews, "The Use of Books," *Library Journal,* 32:249–53 (June 1907); William W. Bishop, "The Theory of Reference Work," *ALA Bulletin,* 9:134–39 (July 1915).

27. Walter B. Briggs, "Reference Work in Public and College Libraries," *Library Journal,* 32:492–95 (Nov. 1907); Willard Austen, "Educational Value of

Reference Room Training for Students," *ALA Bulletin*, 1:274–77 (July 1907); William W. Bishop, "The Amount of Help To Be Given to Readers," *ALA Bulletin*, 2:327–32 (Sept. 1908).

28. U.S. Office of Education, *Biennial Survey of Education in the United States, 1954–1956: Chapter 1* (Washington, D.C.: Govt. Print. Off., 1959), p.30–32.

29. William W. Bishop, "The True Significance of Library Work," *Library Journal*, 42:385–86 (May 1917); Sarah C. N. Bogle, "Preparedness To Meet New Educational Demands," *ALA Bulletin*, 11:153–56 (Sept. 1917); W. Dawson Johnston, "The Library as a Reinforcement of the School," *Public Libraries*, 16:131–34 (April 1911); William I. Fletcher, "Anticipations for the Future of Library Work," *Public Libraries*, 14:1–5 (Jan. 1909).

30. Chamberlain, *op. cit.*, p.154.

31. Johnston, *op. cit.*, p.131.

32. "Public Library and the School Are Parts of the Educational System," *Pennsylvania Library Notes*, 2:1–2 (July 1909).

33. Frederick Morgan Crunden, "The Library: A Plea for Its Recognition," *Library Journal*, 29:C1-2 (Dec. 1904); Ernest C. Richardson, "President's Address," *Library Journal*, 30:C8 (Sept. 1905); Walter L. Brown, "President's Address," *ALA Bulletin*, 11:94 (Sept. 1917).

34. Louis Round Wilson, "Library as an Educator," *Library Journal*, 35:9–10 (Jan. 1910); Canfield, *loc. cit.*

35. Henry E. Legler, "President's Address," *ALA Bulletin*, 7:79–80 (July 1913); J. Maud Campbell, "Educational Opportunity and the Library," *Library Journal*, 32:157–58 (April 1907); James H. Canfield, "Library in Relation to Special Classes of Readers," *Library Journal*, 31:C65–67 (Aug. 1906).

36. Marguerite Reid and John G. Moulton, comps., *Aids in Library Work with Foreigners* (Chicago: American Library Association, 1912); J. Maud Campbell, "Public Library and the Immigrant," *New York Libraries*, 1:132–36 (July–Oct. 1908); John Foster Carr, "Some of the People We Work For," *ALA Bulletin*, 10:149–54 (July 1916).

37. Isabel E. Lord, "Fixing a Purpose," *ALA Bulletin*, 2:165–67 (Sept. 1908); Clinton R. Woodruff, "Education through Free Lectures," *Public Libraries*, 10:346–50 (July 1905); Frank C. Patten, "Library and the Lecture," *Public Libraries*, 11:489–92 (Nov. 1906); Kate L. Roberts, "Club Women and Programs," *Public Libraries*, 14:205–8 (June 1909).

38. Putnam, "The Relation of Free Public Libraries to the Community," *North American Review*, 499:664–65 (June 1898).

39. Edwin W. Gaillard, "University Education in Two Weeks," *Library Journal*, 28:8 (Jan. 1903).

40. Walter L. Brown, "The Changing Public," *Library Journal*, 42:588 (Aug. 1917).

41. John H. Leete, *The Function of the Public Library in a Democracy: An Address* (Pittsburgh: Carnegie Library of Pittsburgh, 1920), p.4.

42. William Warner Bishop, *The Backs of Books and Other Essays in Librarianship* (Baltimore: Williams & Wilkins, 1926), p.197.

43. Although more attention was directed toward the educational objective during the next three decades by the American Library Association, this order of emphasis, in terms of library *practice*, did not change to any marked degree. This conclusion is based on an examination of library literature covering the period from 1920 to 1950. See also Bernard Berelson, *The Library's Public* (New York: Columbia Univ. Pr., 1949), p.55–69, 131; Robert D. Leigh, *The Public Library in the United States* (New York: Columbia Univ. Pr., 1950), p.12–24; and Lester Asheim, ed., *A Forum on the Public Library*

Inquiry (New York: Columbia Univ. Pr., 1950), p.60–65. Therefore, the recreation and reference objectives of public libraries will not be discussed at any length in the following two chapters.

44. Theodore W. Koch, *Books in the War* (Boston: Houghton, 1919).

45. Bishop, "President's Address: The American Library Association at the Crossroads," *ALA Bulletin,* 13:101 (July 1919).

Chapter IV
Serving the Individual, 1920–1940

1. William S. Learned, *The American Public Library and the Diffusion of Knowledge* (New York: Harcourt, 1924).

2. "After-War Library Service," *Public Libraries,* 25:72 (Feb. 1920).

3. Carl H. Milam, "Adult Self-Education," *Public Libraries,* 25:182–84 (April 1920).

4. ———— "The Enlarged Program: Letter to Regional and State Directors," *Public Libraries,* 25:517 (Nov. 1920).

5. The term "adult education" first appeared in the *Readers' Guide* of 1915–1916.

6. American Library Association, *Libraries and Adult Education* (Chicago: The Association, 1926), p.221–46; John Chancellor, ed., *Helping Adults To Learn* (Chicago: American Library Association, 1939), p.28.

7. Learned, *op. cit.,* p.12.

8. *Ibid.,* p.53.

9. One of Learned's recommendations was that funds should be provided to continue the work of the American Library Association in adult education: "Probably in no other group of professional workers is it possible, at one stroke, to reach and so profoundly to effect an important public service. This is partly because it is not a large group, partly because it is inherently a homogeneous and unified group, but largely because it is so disposed and organized as to facilitate from a common center operations of great material and practical benefit on an extensive scale" (*ibid.,* p.76).

10. Morse A. Cartwright, "The American Association for Adult Education," *Adult Education and the Library,* 3:93–94 (Oct. 1928).

11. American Library Association, *op. cit.,* p.7.

12. C. F. D. Belden, Librarian, Boston Public Library; W. W. Bishop, Librarian, University of Michigan Library, Ann Arbor; W. O. Carson, Inspector of Public Libraries, Toronto, Canada; Linda A. Eastman, Librarian, Cleveland Public Library; M. S. Dudgeon, Librarian, Milwaukee Public Library; C. E. Rush, Librarian, Indianapolis Public Library.

13. Judson T. Jennings, "Sticking to Our Last," *ALA Bulletin,* 18:153–56 (Aug. 1924).

14. American Library Association, *Adult Education and the Library,* 1:8 (Nov. 1924).

15. John Chancellor, "Libraries and Adult Education," in Dorothy Rowden, ed., *Handbook of Adult Education in the United States* (New York: American Association for Adult Education, 1936), p.77–78.

16. Emma Felsenthal, *Readable Books in Many Subjects: A Study and a List* (Chicago: American Library Association, 1929), 32p.

17. American Library Association, *Libraries and Adult Education* (Chicago: The Association, 1926), p.249–50.

18. ———— "Papers and Proceedings, Fifty-first Annual Conference, 1929," *ALA Bulletin*, 23:257–60 (Aug. 1929).
19. Edward F. Stevens, "Adult Erudition," *Libraries* (a former publication of Library Bureau, Remington Office Systems, Division of Sperry Rand Corp.), 34:252 (June 1929).
20. John M. Chancellor, "Ten Years of Adult Education," *ALA Bulletin*, 28:278 (May 1935).
21. American Library Association, *Libraries and Adult Education* (Chicago: The Association, 1926), 284p.
22. *Ibid.*, p.7.
23. *Ibid.*, p.107.
24. William E. Henry, "The ALA and Adult Education," *Library Journal*, 50:212 (March 1, 1925).
25. Eduard C. Lindeman, "Adult Education: A Creative Opportunity," *Library Journal*, 50:447 (May 15, 1925).
26. Herman H. B. Meyer, "Library Extension: A Movement or a Problem," *Library Journal*, 50:575 (July 15, 1925).
27. Charles F. D. Belden, "Looking Forward," *ALA Bulletin*, 20:275 (Papers and Proceedings, 48th Meeting, 1926).
28. Melvil Dewey, "Our Next Half-Century," *Library Journal*, 51:889 (Oct. 15, 1926).
29. American Library Association, "The Library and Adult Education, 1924–1934," *ALA Bulletin*, 29:316–17 (June 1935).
30. "Board on the Library and Adult Education," *ALA Bulletin*, 21:194 (July 1927).
31. George H. Locke, "President's Address," *ALA Bulletin*, 21:267 (Oct. 1927).
32. Carl B. Roden, "Ten Years," *Library Journal*, 53:523 (June 15, 1928).
33. In 1934, this same question was discussed at length by J. Periam Danton ("A Plea for a Philosophy of Librarianship," *Library Quarterly*, 4:527–51 [Oct. 1934]).
34. Francis K. W. Drury, "Six Years' Activity in Adult Education," *ALA Bulletin*, 25:35 (Jan. 1931).
35. *Ibid.*, p.36.
36. "The onset of the Depression is usually dated from the fall of 1929. But it was not felt in many cities until 1931, the date of the international slump; and the stock market did not reach its lowest points until 1932 and 1933 . . . municipal institutions did not begin reducing budgets generally until 1931 . . . but by 1935 there was a definite and general improvement in the library expenditures" (Margaret M. Herdman, "The Public Library in Depression," *Library Quarterly*, 13:310–11 [Oct. 1943]).
37. American Library Association, "The Library and Adult Education, 1924–1934," *ALA Bulletin*, 29:318 (June 1935).
38. "Adult Education Board News," *ALA Bulletin*, 31:516 (Sept. 30, 1937).
39. "Adult Education Board," *ALA Bulletin*, 32:570 (Sept. 1938).
40. *Ibid.*, 33:561 (Sept. 1939).
41. American Library Association, *Experiments in Educational Service for Adults* (Chicago: The Association, 1940). (mimeographed)
42. Alice S. Taylor, "Some Aspects of Library Progress," *Library Journal*, 46:588 (July 1921); Virginia Cleaver Bacon, "Possibilities of Informal Education under Library Guidance," *Library Journal*, 52:810–11 (Sept. 1, 1927); Linda A. Eastman, "Part of the Library in Adult Education," *Journal of the American Association of University Women*, 22:68–71 (Jan. 1929).
43. Gratia A. Countryman, "Building for the Future," *ALA Bulletin*, 27:383–84

(July 1934); Robert Hoppock, "Occupational Information Service," *ALA Bulletin,* 27:343–44 (Aug. 1933); Hazel E. Ohman, "Public Library's Place in Providing Job Information," *Special Libraries,* 26:249–53 (Nov. 1935); Linda A. Eastman, "The Part of the City Library in the Vocational Guidance of Adults," *ALA Bulletin,* 26:10–16 (Jan. 1932); Harry D. Kitson, *Vocational Guidance through the Library* (Chicago: American Library Association, 1931).

44. Isaac A. Yabroff, "Indoctrinating for Democracy," *Junior Librarian,* 1:11–12 (Nov. 1939); E. Kathleen Jones, "Trends in Reading Today," *Bulletin of the New Hampshire Public Libraries,* 32:74–77 (Sept. 1936); Evelyn Steel Little, "Power of Books in a Democracy," *Library Journal,* 64:441–45 (June 1, 1939); William H. Carlson, "Preparers of the Mind and Heart," *Library Journal,* 61:182–85 (March 1, 1936).

45. Archibald MacLeish, "Libraries in the Contemporary Crisis," *Library Journal,* 64:879–82 (Nov. 15, 1939); American Library Association, "A National Plan for Libraries," *ALA Bulletin,* 33:138 (Feb. 1939).

46. American Library Association, *Libraries and Adult Education* (Chicago: The Association, 1926), p.221–48.

47. John Chancellor, ed., *Helping Adults To Learn* (Chicago: American Library Association, 1939), p.28.

48. Hazel Webster Byrnes, "The Library Movement in the United States," *Franklin Lectures,* 1:62 (July 1935).

49. William S. Gray and Ruth Munroe, *The Reading Interests and Habits of Adults* (New York: Macmillan, 1929).

50. Douglas Waples and Ralph W. Tyler, *What People Want To Read About* (Chicago: Univ. of Chicago Pr., 1931).

51. Douglas Waples, "The Relation of Subject Interests to Actual Reading," *Library Quarterly,* 2:42–70 (Jan. 1932); Leon Carnovsky, "A Study of the Relationship between Reading Interest and Actual Reading," *Library Quarterly,* 4:76–100 (Jan. 1934).

52. William S. Gray and Bernice E. Leary, *What Makes a Book Readable* (Chicago: Univ. of Chicago Pr., 1935).

53. Lyman L. Bryson, "Readability Laboratory," *Library Journal,* 61:445 (June 1, 1936); "Readable Books for the People," *Publishers Weekly,* 135:778–79 (Feb. 18, 1939).

54. John Chancellor, "The Next Years in Adult Education: Eleventh Annual Report of the Board on the Library and Adult Education, for Ten Months Ending January 31, 1936," *ALA Bulletin,* 30:331 (May 1936); *Helping Adults To Learn* (Chicago: American Library Association, 1939), p.28–32.

55. Harrison W. Craver, "Unfinished Business," *ALA Bulletin,* 32:418 (July 1938).

56. Carleton B. Joeckel, ed., *Current Issues in Library Administration: Papers Presented before the Library Institute at the University of Chicago, August 1–12, 1938* (Chicago: Univ. of Chicago Pr., 1939), p.26–27.

57. John Chancellor and Chester S. Williams, *Printed Page and the Public Platform: A Study of the Relation of Reading to Forums and Discussion* (Washington, D.C.: Govt. Print. Off., 1938).

58. American Library Association, *Libraries and Adult Education* (Chicago: The Association, 1926), p.37.

59. Elta Lenart, "Discussion Groups," *Adult Education and the Library,* 5:49 (April 1930).

60. *Ibid.,* p.35–52; Ruth Rutzen, "Detroit's Adult Education Service," *ALA Bulletin,* 31:150 (March 1937).

61. John Chancellor, "The Next Years in Adult Education: Eleventh Annual Report of the Board on the Library and Adult Education, for Ten Months Ending January 31, 1936," *ALA Bulletin,* 30:335 (May 1936).

62. —— and Williams *op. cit.,* p.79.

63. Alvin Johnson, *The Public Library—A People's University* (New York: American Association for Adult Education, 1938), p.67–68, 76.

64. Carleton B. Joeckel and Leon Carnovsky, *A Metropolitan Library in Action* (Chicago: Univ. of Chicago Pr., 1940), p.350.

65. Public library expenditures were 20 percent less in 1933 than in 1930 (Herdman, *op. cit.,* p.319).

66. American Library Association, "Standards for Public Libraries," *ALA Bulletin,* 27:513 (Nov. 1933).

67. Ralph Munn, "Library Objectives," *ALA Bulletin,* 30:586 (Aug. 1936).

68. Louis R. Wilson, "The Next Fifty Years," *Library Journal,* 61:256 (April 1, 1936).

69. J. Periam Danton, *op. cit.,* p.545; Munn, *op. cit.,* p.584; Wilson, *loc. cit.*

70. American Library Association, "A National Plan for Libraries," *ALA Bulletin,* 33:138 (Feb. 1939).

71. Joeckel, *op. cit.,* p.40.

72. Cecil McHale, "Paper Presented at the ALA Lending Section (Proceedings of the American Library Association)," *ALA Bulletin,* 34:139–43 (Aug. 1940).

73. Mary L. Ely, ed., *Adult Education in Action* (New York: American Association for Adult Education, 1936), p.253.

74. Robert A. Miller, "Search for Fundamentals," *Library Journal,* 61:298 (April 15, 1936).

75. Emily M. Danton, ed., *The Library of Tomorrow* (Chicago: American Library Association, 1939), p.158.

76. American Library Association, "A National Plan for Libraries," *ALA Bulletin,* 33:138 (Feb. 1939).

77. *Ibid.,* p.140–41.

78. Louis R. Wilson, "Restudying the Library Chart," *ALA Bulletin,* 30:485 (June 1936).

79. Joeckel, ed., *op. cit.,* p.72–73.

80. Johnson, *op. cit.*

81. *Ibid.,* p.73.

82. American Library Association, *Libraries and Adult Education* (Chicago: The Association, 1926), p.27.

83. Matthew S. Dudgeon, "Informal Report of the Board on the Library and Adult Education," *ALA Bulletin,* 22:337 (Sept. 1928).

84. John Cotton Dana, "Thoughts on the Library and Adult Education," *Library Journal,* 53:945 (Nov. 15, 1928).

85. "The First Institute on Adult Education through the Library," *Adult Education and the Library,* 4:83 (July 1929).

86. Arthur E. Bostwick, *The American Public Library* (New York: D. Appleton, 1929), p.376.

87. Ernestine Rose, *Adult Education: Suggestive Aids for Libraries* (New York: New York Library Association, 1935), p.2.

88. Louis R. Wilson, ed., *Library Trends: Papers Presented before the Library Institute at the University of Chicago, August 3–15, 1936* (Chicago: Univ. of Chicago Pr., 1937), p.133.

89. "Adult Education Board," *ALA Bulletin,* 31:512 (Sept. 1937).

90. American Library Association, "A National Plan for Libraries," *ALA Bulletin,* 33:141 (Feb. 1939).
91. John Chancellor, ed., *Helping Adults To Learn* (Chicago: American Library Association, 1939), p.182–83.
92. *Ibid.,* p.198.

Chapter V
Strengthening Democracy, 1941–1956

1. American Library Association, *The Library—1941: A Policy Statement Adopted by the Council of the American Library Association* (Chicago: The Association, 1941). (leaflet)
2. Nell A. Unger, Katherine Shorey, and others, *National Defense and the Public Library* (Chicago: American Library Association, 1942).
3. American Library Association, *Victory Book Campaign, 1942–1943* (Chicago: American Library Association, 1944). (mimeographed)
4. Carl Vitz, "Pleasure and Regret," *ALA Bulletin,* 39:231–32 (July 1945).
5. American Library Association Council, "Four Year Goals: Statement of Policy Adopted by Council, January 31, 1948," *ALA Bulletin,* 42:122 (March 1948).
6. Len Arnold, "The ALA 75th Anniversary Conference: A Report of the General Sessions," *ALA Bulletin,* 45:269–71 (Sept. 1951).
7. Library Bill of Rights, adopted by the ALA Council, June 18, 1948, and amended by the Council, February 1, 1961.
8. Resolution Protesting Loyalty Investigations in Libraries, adopted by the ALA Council, June 18, 1948.
9. John J. Boll, *The American Library Association and Intellectual Freedom* ("Occasional Papers," No.35 [Urbana: Univ. of Illinois Library School, 1953]).
10. American Library Association, Committee on Post-War Planning, *Post-War Standards for Public Libraries* (Chicago: The Association, 1943), 92p.
11. *Ibid.,* p.20.
12. *Ibid.,* p.22–23.
13. Cyril O. Houle, "A Basic Philosophy of Library Service for Adult Education: Part I," *Library Journal,* 71:1514–15 (Nov. 1, 1946).
14. Joseph L. Wheeler, *Progress and Problems in Education for Librarianship* (New York: Carnegie Corp., 1946), p.11–12.
15. Herbert Goldhor, "Sees Public Library Work Entering New Phase," *Library Journal,* 72:1775 (Dec. 15, 1947).
16. Robert D. Leigh, *The Public Library in the United States* (New York: Columbia Univ. Pr., 1950), p.223.
17. *Ibid.,* p.48–49.
18. Emerson Greenaway, "Setting the Course for the Next Decade," *Public Libraries,* 4:9–13 (March 1950); Raymond C. Lindquist, "If Not the People's University—Then What?," *Public Libraries,* 4:3 (March 1950); Ralph A. Ulveling, "Moving Forward as the People's University," *Public Libraries,* 4:13–16 (March 1950).
19. Jesse H. Shera, Dean of the Library School at Western Reserve University, wrote: "The misconceptions that underlie both the adult education movement and the Public Library Inquiry derive from the same fallacious definition of the educational function of the library.

Only in a few isolated instances has personal contact between patron and librarian made possible the student-teacher relationship; yet from just such exceptions has grown a whole myth concerning the educational role of the librarian in society. So long as the social responsibility of the librarian remains the collecting, organizing, servicing, and administering of the graphic records of civilization and the encouragement of their most effective utilization, he cannot be an educator in the proper sense. To superimpose upon his established functions these irrelevant tasks will certainly confuse his objectives, if it does not actually destroy the true purpose for which the library was created. . . . To reason that, because educators and librarians both make use of books and ideas, librarians are therefore educators is equivalent to saying that Old Dutch Cleanser is a food merely because it is usually kept in the kitchen and used by the cook" ("On the Value of Library History," *Library Quarterly*, 22:246–47 [July 1952]). In 1954, Mrs. Grace T. Stevenson, Associate Executive Secretary of the American Library Association, answered Shera's charge (Wisconsin Free Library Commission, *Proceedings of the Sixth Institute on Public Library Management: Informal Education through Libraries* [Madison: The Commission, 1955], p.48. (mimeographed)

20. Cyril O. Houle, *Libraries in Adult and Fundamental Education* (Paris: United Nations Educational, Scientific, and Cultural Organization, 1951), p.22–23.
21. Lester Asheim, ed., *A Forum on the Public Library Inquiry: The Conference at the University of Chicago Graduate Library School, August 8–13, 1949* (New York: Columbia Univ. Pr., 1950), p.63.
22. ———— *Training Needs of Librarians Doing Adult Education Work: A Report of the Allerton Park Conference, November 14–16, 1954* (Chicago: American Library Association, 1955), p.8–9.
23. ———— *A Forum on the Public Library Inquiry* (New York: Columbia Univ. Pr., 1950), p.276.
24. *Ibid.*, p.255.
25. *Ibid.*, p.47.
26. Lowell A. Martin, "Library Service to Adults," *Library Quarterly*, 25:12 (Jan. 1955).
27. American Library Association, Public Libraries Division, Co-ordinating Committee on Revision of Public Library Standards, *Public Library Service: A Guide to Evaluation, with Minimum Standards* (Chicago: The Association, 1956), p.4.
28. The library's educational goals are discussed on p.82.
29. In 1950, Robert Leigh, in the summary volume of the Public Library Inquiry, reported that it was the "provision of materials for existing formal and informal groups in the community which constitutes the great bulk of the adult education activity of most public libraries at the present time," but the public library, he added, did not "serve as the officially designated library for the existing major agencies of formal adult education." Leigh's conclusion was based on a study of sixty public libraries (Leigh, *op. cit.*, p.105–8). In 1954, in the ALA survey, *Adult Education Activities in Public Libraries*, it was stated that 457 of the 1,692 libraries surveyed provided services to other adult educational agencies (Helen Lyman Smith, *Adult Education Activities in Public Libraries: A Report of the ALA Survey of Adult Education Activities in Public Libraries and State Library Extension Agencies of the United States* [Chicago: American Library Association, 1954], p.35).

30. R. N. O'Reilly, "Library Evangelism and the Educational Functions of the Public Library," *Library Quarterly,* 17:25 (Jan. 1947).

31. American Library Association, Committee on Post-War Planning, *Post-War Standards for Public Libraries* (Chicago: The Association, 1943), p.28–29.

32. Carleton B. Joeckel and Amy Winslow, *A National Plan for Public Library Service* (Chicago: American Library Association, 1948).

33. *Ibid.,* p.4, 16.

34. Ralph A. Beals, "The Public Library as an Agency for General Education," in Nelson B. Henry, ed., *The Library in General Education: Forty-second Yearbook of the National Society for the Study of Education, Part II* (Chicago: Univ. of Chicago Pr., 1943), p.107; Lowell Martin, "Community Analysis for the Library," in Leon Carnovsky and Lowell Martin, eds., *The Library in the Community: Papers Presented before the Library Institute at the University of Chicago, August 23–28, 1943* (Chicago: Univ. of Chicago Pr., 1944), p.201–14.

35. The aims of the ALA Library-Community Project were to provide leadership, stimulation, and professional assistance to enable libraries to develop long-term adult educational programs based on an analysis of community needs.

36. American Library Association, Public Libraries Division, Co-ordinating Committee on Revision of Public Library Standards, *op. cit.,* p.25–30; ALA Library-Community Project Headquarters Staff, *Studying the Community* (Chicago: American Library Association, 1960).

37. Archibald MacLeish, *A Time To Speak* (Boston: Houghton, 1941), p.150; Leon Carnovsky and Lowell Martin, eds., *op. cit.,* p.2–6; Myra Kolitsch, "Toward a Philosophy of Librarianship," *Library Quarterly,* 15:27 (Jan. 1945); ALA Council, "Four Year Goals: Statement of Policy Adopted by Council, January 31, 1948," *ALA Bulletin,* 42:122 (March 1948); E. W. McDiarmid, "A Crusade for an Educated America," *ALA Bulletin,* 42:289–93 (July–Aug. 1948).

38. ALA Adult Education Board, "Adult Education Policy for Libraries," *ALA Bulletin,* 38:451–52 (Nov. 1944); Mary U. Rothrock, "Libraries in a New Era," *ALA Bulletin,* 40:228 (July 1946); Flora Belle Ludington, "Taproot, Trunk, and Branches," *ALA Bulletin,* 47:372 (Aug. 1953).

39. Joeckel and Winslow, *op. cit.,* p.1–2; Carl H. Milam, "Notes on Adult Education," *ALA Bulletin,* 40:213 (June 1946); Helen Haines, *Living with Books: The Art of Book Selection* (New York: Columbia Univ. Pr., 1950), p.15.

40. O'Reilly, *loc. cit.*

41. Smith, *op. cit.,* p.10.

42. Lowell A. Martin, "Library Service to Adults," *Library Quarterly,* 25:10 (Jan. 1955).

43. "Adult Education Board," *ALA Bulletin,* 38:341 (Oct. 1, 1944).

44. Smith, *op. cit.,* p.36; Fern Long, "Work with Community Groups," *New Jersey Library Bulletin,* 13:11–28 (June 1945); Miriam E. McNally, "Adult Education Works Two Ways," *Library Journal,* 73:1053–59 (Aug. 1948); Thomas Barenfeld, "Clubs Depend on Libraries," *Library Journal,* 77:112–14 (Jan. 15, 1952); "One Librarian to Another: Public Library Gives Program Help," *Wisconsin Library Bulletin,* 50:193–94 (Sept.–Oct. 1954).

45. Smith, *op. cit.,* p.41; Fern Long and Clara Lucioli, "Live Long and Like It Club: A Project in Adult Education for Older People," *Wilson Library Bulletin,* 23:301-5 (Dec. 1948); Winston R. Henderson, "Orlando's Family Coun-

cil Series," *Florida Libraries*, 5:16 (June 1954); Verna Nistendirk, "Boonslick Did It," *ALA Bulletin*, 49:565–67 (Nov. 1955); William Shank, "Music
to Queens' Taste," *ALA Bulletin*, 49:16–17 (Jan. 1955).

46. Kate Coplan, "Baltimore's Atomic Energy Institute," *Library Journal*,
72:367–70 (May 1, 1947).

47. The purpose of the ALA Adult Education Subgrant Project (1953–1954)
was to stimulate the development of educational services to adult—and
young adult—community groups through libraries, thereby giving libraries
an opportunity to initiate new programs or to develop current ones, and to
demonstrate the fitness and ability of libraries to present meaningful and
vigorous adult educational services to groups *(Experimental Projects in
Adult Education: A Report of the ALA Adult Education Subgrant Project*
[Chicago: American Library Association, 1956], p.4).

48. ALA Adult Education Board, *loc. cit.*

49. John Walker Powell, "One Step Nearer Leadership: Guided Group Reading
as a Library Service," *Library Journal*, 71:443–49 (April 1, 1946); *Education
for Maturity* (New York: Hermitage House, 1949), p.90–94.

50. Lowell A. Martin, "Guided Group Reading as a Library Service: The
Chicago Project," *Library Journal*, 71:734–39 (May 15, 1946).

51. American Library Association, "The Great Issues," *The Booklist*, 44:397
(Aug. 1948).

52. "American Heritage Project at Work," *Wilson Library Bulletin*, 27:437–47
(Feb. 1953); American Library Association. *American Heritage Project Annual Report, 1954–55* (Chicago: The Association, 1956).

53. Mrs. G. E. Miller and Ruth Warncke, "Aspects of an Experiment in Adult
Education," *Michigan Librarian*, 3:6–8 (March 1947); Mary Knorr, "Plan-
ning a Program Planning Institute," *New Mexico Library Bulletin*, 23:3–6
(Oct. 1954); Grace Stevenson, "Libraries Can Help Clubs with Planning
Programs," *Library News Bulletin of the Washington State Library*, 16:450–
52 (July 1946); American Library Association, Adult Education Section,
Prospecting for Library Patrons (Chicago: The Association, 1950), p.11–15.

54. Ruth Warncke, "Public Libraries," *Rural Social Systems and Adult Education;* a Committee Report by Charles P. Loomis *et al.* (Lansing, Mich.:
Michigan State College Pr., 1953).

55. Smith, *op. cit.*, p.xi, 3.

56. Warncke, *op. cit.*, p.176–79.

57. Smith, *op. cit.*, p.11–16.

58. Wheeler, *op. cit.*, p.15.

59. Beals, *op. cit.*, p.10.

60. O'Reilly, *op. cit.*, p.21.

61. Lowell A. Martin, "Library Service to Adults," *Library Quarterly*, 25:12
(Jan. 1955).

62. Beals, *op. cit.*, p.11.

63. Asheim, *A Forum on the Public Library Inquiry* (New York: Columbia
Univ. Pr., 1950), p.48.

64. Harold L. Hamill, "Boon or Booby Trap," *ALA Bulletin*, 48:210–14 (April
1954).

65. Emerson Greenaway, "Two Points of View," *ALA Bulletin*, 48:214–17 (April
1954).

66. O'Reilly, *op. cit.*, p.24; Chase Dane, "How Much Adult Education," *Illinois
Libraries*, 37:64–68 (Feb. 1954).

67. John Chancellor, quoted in Wayne Shirley's "What Happened to Our Adult

Education Hopes," *Library Journal* 72:1506 (Nov. 1, 1947); Cyril O. Houle, "New Leadership in the Library," *ALA Bulletin,* 35:159 (March 1941).

Chapter VI
Moving Forward, 1957–1964

1. American Library Association, Public Libraries Division, Co-ordinating Committee on Revision of Public Library Standards, *Public Library Service: A Guide to Evaluation, with Minimum Standards* (Chicago: The Association, 1956). 74p.
2. Ralph Munn, "Planning for Cooperation," *ALA Bulletin,* 58:497 (June 1964).
3. Ruth P. Tubby, "Planning for the Long Haul toward Meeting Standards," *ALA Bulletin,* 58:499 (June 2, 1964).
4. John G. Lorenz and Rose Vainstein, "Emerging Trends of Library Organization," in Roberta Bowler, ed., *Local Public Library Administration* (Chicago: International City Managers' Assn., 1964), p.35–36.
5. American Library Association, *Student Use of Libraries: An Inquiry into the Needs of Students, Libraries, and the Educational Process* (Chicago: The Association, 1964).
6. Lowell A. Martin, *Students and the Pratt Library: Challenge and Opportunity* (Baltimore: Enoch Pratt Free Library, 1963).
7. "Review and Evaluation of *Access to Public Libraries";* a Report to the Executive Board and Council of the American Library Association from the Board of Directors of the Library Administration Division, January 26, 1964, p.7.
8. *Access to Public Libraries: A Research Project;* prepared for the Library Administration Division, American Library Association, by International Research Associates, Inc. (Chicago: American Library Association, 1963), p.1–68.
9. Eleanor Phinney, "Library Service to an Aging Population," *ALA Bulletin,* 51:607–9 (Sept. 1957); "Trends in Library Services to the Aging," *ALA Bulletin,* 53:534–35 (June 1959).
10. *State Library Activities in the Field of Aging: Survey Report for the Adult Services Division Committee on Library Service to an Aging Population,* by Virginia Owens (Chicago: American Library Association. Adult Services Division, March 1960). 12p. (mimeographed)
11. Ruth Warncke, *The Library-Community Project of the American Library Association: Report 1955–1960* (Chicago: The Association, 1960), p.124–27. (mimeographed)
12. American Library Association, Library-Community Project Headquarters Staff, *Studying the Community: A Basis for Planning Library Adult Education Services* (Chicago: The Association, 1960).
13. Eleanor Phinney, "Focussing Library Services on Community Needs," *Librarianship and Adult Needs* (Syracuse, N.Y.: Syracuse Univ. School of Library Science, 1963), p.40.
14. Ruth W. Gregory, "Adult Education Services in Public Libraries—1959," *ALA Bulletin,* 53:788 (Oct. 1959).
15. *Ibid.,* p.790.
16. *Ibid.,* p.789, 791.
17. Marie D. Wann and Marthine V. Woodward, *Participation in Adult Education: A Statistical Analysis of the Adult Education Data Obtained in the*

October, 1957 Current Population Survey of the Bureau of Census (Washington, D.C.: Govt. Print. Off., 1959).

18. Eleanor Phinney, "Recent Trends in Public Library Adult Services," *ALA Bulletin,* 57:262–63 (March 1963).

19. Ethel Bruya, "Recent Activities of Maryland Libraries and Librarians in the Field of Aging," *Maryland Libraries,* Winter, 1961, p.19.

20. Eleanor Phinney, *A Study of Current Practices in Public Library Service to an Aging Population: An Evaluative Report* ("Occasional Papers," No. 62 [Univ. of Illinois Graduate Library School, Nov. 1961]).

21. Gregory, *op. cit.,* p.791.

Chapter VII
Summary and Conclusions

1. In 1959, Jerome Cushman wrote: "The library is going to have to decide upon some identification of terms or it will be diverted from its chance, now only a hope, to help provide for educational experiences which are in keeping with its traditional role" ("Library Services to Adult Education in the Smaller Community," *Library Trends,* 7:45 [July 1959]).

2. Derived from an appraisal and analysis of the needs and interests of the community.

3. The most comprehensive research study of the continuing learner is Cyril O. Houle's *The Inquiring Mind: A Study of the Adult Who Continues To Learn* (Madison, Wis.: Univ. of Wisconsin Pr., 1961). This work discusses the types and activities of continuing learners and suggests the reasons why they continue their learning.

4. John W. C. Johnstone, *Volunteers for Learning* (Chicago: National Opinion Research Center, 1963).

5. Robert D. Leigh, *The Public Library in the United States: General Report of the Public Library Inquiry* (New York: Columbia Univ. Pr., 1950), p.48–49.

A Selective
Bibliography

(For some of the major contributions to the literature of library adult education during the period 1956–1964, see the special bibliography on pages 102–4.)

Books

American Library Association. *Libraries and Adult Education*. Chicago: The Association, 1926.

——— Committee on Post-War Planning. *Post-War Standards for Public Libraries*. Chicago: The Association, 1943.

——— Library-Community Project Headquarters Staff. *Studying the Community: A Basis for Planning Library Adult Education Services*. Chicago: The Association, 1960.

——— Public Libraries Division. Co-ordinating Committee on Revision of Public Library Standards. *Public Library Service: A Guide to Evaluation, with Minimum Standards*. Chicago: The Association, 1956.

Asheim, Lester, ed. *A Forum on the Public Library Inquiry: The Conference at the University of Chicago Graduate Library School, August 8–13, 1949*. New York: Columbia Univ. Pr., 1950.

Beals, Ralph A. "The Public Library as an Agency for General Education," in Nelson B. Henry, ed., *The Library in General Education: Forty-second Yearbook of the National Society for the Study of Education, Part II*. Chicago: Univ. of Chicago Pr., 1943.

Berelson, Bernard. *The Library's Public*. New York: Columbia Univ. Pr., 1949.

Bostwick, Arthur E. *The American Public Library*. New York: D. Appleton, 1929.

———— ed. *The Library and Society: Reprints of Papers and Addresses.* New York: Wilson, 1920.

———— ed. *Popular Libraries of the World.* Chicago: American Library Association, 1933.

Carnovsky, Leon, and Martin, Lowell, eds. *The Library in the Community: Papers Presented before the Library Institute at the University of Chicago, August 23–28, 1943.* Chicago: Univ. of Chicago Pr., 1944.

Chancellor, John, ed. *Helping Adults To Learn.* Chicago: American Library Association, 1939.

———— "Libraries and Adult Education," in Dorothy Rowden, ed., *Handbook of Adult Education in the United States.* New York: American Association for Adult Education, 1936.

———— and Williams, Chester S. *Printed Page and the Public Platform: A Study of the Relation of Reading to Forums and Discussion.* Washington, D.C.: Govt. Print. Off., 1938.

Danton, Emily M., ed. *The Library of Tomorrow.* Chicago: American Library Association, 1939.

Ditzion, Sidney. *Arsenals of a Democratic Culture.* Chicago: American Library Association, 1947.

Ely, Mary L., ed. *Adult Education in Action.* New York: American Association for Adult Education, 1936.

Felsenthal, Emma. *Readable Books in Many Subjects: A Study and a List.* Chicago: American Library Association, 1929.

Flexner, Jennie M., and Edge, Sigrid A. *A Readers' Advisory Service.* New York: American Association for Adult Education, 1934.

Gray, William S., and Leary, Bernice E. *What Makes a Book Readable.* Chicago: Univ. of Chicago Pr., 1935.

———— and Munroe, Ruth. *The Reading Interests and Habits of Adults.* New York: Macmillan, 1929.

Hendrick, Burton J. *The Life of Andrew Carnegie.* New York: Doubleday, Doran, 1932.

Houle, Cyril O. *Libraries in Adult and Fundamental Education.* Paris: United Nations Educational, Scientific, and Cultural Organization, 1951.

Joeckel, Carleton B., ed. *Current Issues in Library Administration: Papers Presented before the Library Institute at the University of Chicago, August 1–12, 1938.* Chicago: Univ. of Chicago Pr., 1939.

———— and Carnovsky, Leon. *A Metropolitan Library in Action.* Chicago: Univ. of Chicago Pr., 1940.

———— and Winslow, Amy. *A National Plan for Public Library Service.* Chicago: American Library Association, 1948.

Johnson, Alvin. *The Public Library—A People's University.* New York: American Association for Adult Education, 1938.

Kitson, Harry D. *Vocational Guidance through the Library.* Chicago: American Library Association, 1931.

Koch, Theodore W. *A Book of Carnegie Libraries.* New York: Wilson, 1917.

———— *Books in the War.* Boston: Houghton, 1919.

Learned, William S. *The American Public Library and the Diffusion of*

Knowledge. New York: Harcourt, 1924.

Leete, John H. *The Function of the Public Library in a Democracy: An Address.* Pittsburgh: Carnegie Library of Pittsburgh, 1920.

Leigh, Robert D. *The Public Library in the United States: General Report of the Public Library Inquiry.* New York: Columbia Univ. Pr., 1950.

MacLeish, Archibald. *A Time To Speak.* Boston: Houghton, 1941.

Martin, Lowell. "Community Analysis for the Library," in Leon Carnovsky and Lowell Martin, eds., *The Library in the Community: Papers Presented before the Library Institute at the University of Chicago, August 23–28, 1943.* Chicago: Univ. of Chicago Pr., 1944.

Monroe, Margaret Ellen. *Library Adult Education: The Biography of an Idea.* New York: Scarecrow, 1963.

Powell, John Walker. *Education for Maturity.* New York: Hermitage House, 1949.

Reid, Marguerite, and Moulton, John G., comps. *Aids in Library Work with Foreigners.* Chicago: American Library Association, 1912.

Rose, Ernestine. *Adult Education: Suggestive Aids for Libraries.* New York: New York Library Association, 1935.

———— *The Public Library in American Life.* New York: Columbia Univ. Pr., 1954.

Shera, Jesse H. *Foundations of the Public Library.* Chicago: Univ. of Chicago Pr., 1949.

Smith, Albert. *History of the Town of Peterborough, Hillsborough County, New Hampshire.* Boston: George H. Ellis, 1876.

Stevenson, Grace T. "Adult Education in Libraries," in *Handbook of Adult Education in the United States.* Chicago: Adult Education Association of the U.S.A., 1960.

Ticknor, George. *Life, Letters and Journals of George Ticknor.* Boston: James R. Osgood and Co. 1876.

Unger, Nell A., Katherine Shorey, and others. *National Defense and the Public Library.* Chicago: American Library Association, 1942.

U.S. Bureau of Education. *Public Libraries in the United States of America: Their History, Condition, and Management.* Washington, D.C.: Govt. Print. Off., 1876.

Utley, George B. *Fifty Years of the American Library Association.* Chicago: American Library Association, 1926.

Wadlin, Horace G. *The Public Library of the City of Boston: A History.* Boston: Printed at the Library and published by the Trustees, 1911.

Waples, Douglas, and Tyler, Ralph W. *What People Want To Read About.* Chicago: Univ. of Chicago Pr., 1931.

Articles and Periodicals

Adams, Charles Francis, Jr. "Fiction in Public Libraries and Educational Catalogues," *Library Journal,* 4:330–38 (Sept. 1879).

———— "The Public Library and the Public Schools," *Library Journal,* 1:437–41 (Aug. 1877).

"Adult Education Board," *ALA Bulletin,* 32:567–72 (Sept. 1938).

"Adult Education Board," *ALA Bulletin,* 33:558–62 (Sept. 1939).

"Adult Education Board," *ALA Bulletin,* 38:341–42 (Oct. 1, 1944).

"Adult Education Board News," *ALA Bulletin,* 31:510–16 (Sept. 30, 1937).

"American Heritage Project at Work," *Wilson Library Bulletin,* 27:437–47 (Feb. 1953).

American Library Association. *Adult Education and the Library,* 1:8 (Nov. 1924).

———— "The Great Issues," *The Booklist,* 44:397 (Aug. 1948).

———— "A National Plan for Libraries," *ALA Bulletin,* 33:137–50 (Feb. 1939).

———— "The Library and Adult Education, 1924–1934," *ALA Bulletin,* 29:316–23 (June 1935).

———— "Standards for Public Libraries," *ALA Bulletin,* 27:513–14 (Nov. 1933).

American Library Association Council. "Four Year Goals: Statement of Policy Adopted by Council, January 31, 1948," *ALA Bulletin,* 42:121–22 (March 1948).

Bacon, Virginia Cleaver. "Possibilities of Informal Education under Library Guidance," *Library Journal,* 52:810–11 (Sept. 1, 1927).

Billings, John Shaw. "The Public Library: Its Uses to the Municipality," *Library Journal,* 28:293–94 (June 1903).

Birge, Edward A. "Books and Life," *Library Journal,* 31:203–11 (May 1906).

Bishop, William W. "The Amount of Help To Be Given to Readers," *ALA Bulletin,* 2:327–32 (Sept. 1908).

———— "The True Significance of Library Work," *Library Journal,* 42:385–86 (May 1917).

"Board on the Library and Adult Education," *ALA Bulletin,* 21:194–99 (July 1927).

Bogle, Sarah C. N. "Preparedness To Meet New Educational Demands," *ALA Bulletin,* 11:153–56 (Sept. 1917).

Bryson, Lyman L. "Readability Laboratory," *Library Journal,* 61:445 (June 1, 1936).

Byrnes, Hazel Webster. "The Library Movement in the United States," *Franklin Lectures,* 1:48–64 (July 1935).

Campbell, J. Maud. "Educational Opportunity and the Library," *Library Journal,* 32:157–58 (April 1907).

———— "Public Library and the Immigrant," *New York Libraries,* 1:100–105, 129, 132–36 (July–Oct. 1908).

Canfield, James Hulme. "Library in Relation to Special Classes of Readers," *Library Journal,* 31:C65–67 (Aug. 1906).

———— "Library's Part in Education," *Public Libraries,* 14:120 (April 1909).

Carnovsky, Leon. "The Public Library in the U.S.," *Libri,* 2:281–91 (June 1953).

———— "A Study of the Relationship between Reading Interest and Actual Reading," *Library Quarterly*, 4:76–110 (Jan. 1934).

Cartwright, Morse A. "The American Association for Adult Education," *Adult Education and the Library*, 3:93–94 (Oct. 1928).

Chamberlain, Arthur H. "Increasing the Efficiency of the Library as an Educational Factor," *ALA Bulletin*, 5:154–63 (July 1911).

Chancellor, John M. "Ten Years of Adult Education," *ALA Bulletin*, 28:278 (May 1935).

Coplan, Kate. "Baltimore's Atomic Energy Institute," *Library Journal*, 72:367–71 (May 1, 1947).

Cutter, Charles A. "Common Sense in Libraries," *Library Journal*, 14:C1–8 (Sept. 1889).

———— "Should Libraries Buy Only the Best Books or the Best Books That People Will Read," *Library Journal*, 26:69–72 (July 1901).

Dana, John Cotton. "Thoughts on the Library and Adult Education," *Library Journal*, 53:945 (Nov. 15, 1928).

Dane, Chase. "How Much Adult Education," *Illinois Libraries*, 37:64–68 (Feb. 1954).

Danton, J. Periam. "A Plea for a Philosophy of Librarianship," *Library Quarterly*, 4:527–51 (Oct. 1934).

De Vleeschauwer, H. J. "Encyclopedia of Library History," *Mousaion*, 2:1–95 (1955).

Dewey, Melvil. "Field and Future of Travelling Libraries," *Home Education Bulletin* (University of the State of New York, No.40), Sept. 1901, p.6–8.

———— "Libraries as Related to the Educational Work of the States," *Library Notes*, 3:333–40 (Sept. 1888).

———— "The Profession," *Library Journal*, 1:5–6 (Sept. 1876).

Drury, Francis K. W. "Six Years' Activity in Adult Education," *ALA Bulletin*, 25:31–37 (Jan. 1931).

Dudgeon, Matthew S. "Informal Report of the Board on the Library and Adult Education," *ALA Bulletin*, 22:333–37 (Sept. 1928).

Eastman, Linda A. "The Part of the City Library in the Vocational Guidance of Adults," *ALA Bulletin*, 26:10–16 (Jan. 1932).

———— "Part of the Library in Adult Education," *Journal of the American Association of University Women*, 22:68–71 (Jan. 1929).

"The First Institute on Adult Education through the Library," *Adult Education and the Library*, 4:82–84 (July 1929).

Foster, William E. "Methods of Securing the Interest of a Community," *Library Journal*, 5:245–47 (Sept.–Oct. 1880).

———— "The School and the Library: Their Mutual Relations," *Library Journal*, 4:319–25 (Sept. 1879).

Green, Samuel Swett. "Address of the President," *Library Journal*, 16:3–9 (Dec. 1891).

———— "Libraries as Bureaus of Information," *Library Journal*, 21:324–27 (Sept. 1896).

———— "Personal Relations between Librarians and Readers," *Library Journal*, 1:74–81 (Oct. 1876).

Greenaway, Emerson. "Setting the Course for the Next Decade," *Public Libraries,* 4:9–13 (March 1950).

———— "Two Points of View," *ALA Bulletin,* 48:214–17 (April 1954).

Gregory, Ruth W. "Adult Education Services in Public Libraries—1959," *ALA Bulletin,* 53:787–91 (Oct. 1959).

Hamill, Harold L. "Boon or Booby Trap," *ALA Bulletin,* 48:210–14 (April 1954).

Henry, William E. "The ALA and Adult Education," *Library Journal,* 50:211–12 (March 1, 1925).

Herdman, Margaret M. "The Public Library in Depression," *Library Quarterly,* 13:310–34 (Oct. 1943).

Hill, Frank P. "Fiction in Libraries," *Library Journal,* 15:325 (Nov. 1890).

Houle, Cyril O. "A Basic Philosophy of Library Service for Adult Education: Part I," *Library Journal,* 71:1513–17 (Nov. 1, 1946).

Jennings, Judson T. "Sticking to Our Last," *ALA Bulletin,* 18:153–56 (Aug. 1924).

Johnston, W. Dawson. "The Library as a Reinforcement of the School," *Public Libraries,* 16:131–34 (April 1911).

Knorr, Mary. "Planning a Program Planning Institute," *New Mexico Library Bulletin,* 23:3–6 (Oct. 1954).

Lenart, Elta. "Discussion Groups," *Adult Education and the Library,* 5:35–52 (April 1930).

Lindeman, Eduard C. "Adult Education: A Creative Opportunity," *Library Journal,* 50:445–47 (May 15, 1925).

Lindquist, Raymond C. "If Not the People's University—Then What?" *Public Libraries,* 4:3 (March 1950).

Long, Fern. "Work with Community Groups," *New Jersey Library Bulletin,* 13:11–28 (June 1945).

———— and Lucioli, Clara. "Live Long and Like It Club: A Project in Adult Education for Older People," *Wilson Library Bulletin,* 23:301–5 (Dec. 1948).

McDiarmid, E. W. "A Crusade for an Educated America," *ALA Bulletin,* 42:289–93 (July-Aug. 1948).

MacLeish, Archibald. "Libraries in the Contemporary Crisis," *Library Journal,* 64:879–82 (Nov. 15, 1939).

McNally, Miriam E. "Adult Education Works Two Ways," *Library Journal,* 73:1053–59 (Aug. 1948).

Martin, Lowell A. "Guided Group Reading as a Library Service: The Chicago Project," *Library Journal,* 71:734–39 (May 15, 1946).

———— "Library Service to Adults," *Library Quarterly,* 25:1–14 (Jan. 1955).

Miller, Mrs. G. E., and Warncke, Ruth. "Aspects of an Experiment in Adult Education," *Michigan Librarian,* 3:6–8 (March 1947).

Miller, Robert A. "Search for Fundamentals," *Library Journal,* 61:298 (April 15, 1936).

Munn, Ralph. "Library Objectives," *ALA Bulletin,* 30:583–86 (Aug. 1936).

Nistendirk, Verna. "Boonslick Did It," *ALA Bulletin,* 49:565–67 (Nov. 1955).

"One Librarian to Another: Public Library Gives Program Help," *Wisconsin Library Bulletin*, 50:193–94 (Sept.–Oct. 1954).

O'Reilly, R. N. "Library Evangelism and the Educational Functions of the Public Library," *Library Quarterly*, 17:18–27 (Jan. 1947).

Patten, Frank C. "Library and the Lecture," *Public Libraries*, 11:489–92 (Nov. 1906).

Phinney, Eleanor. "Recent Trends in Public Library Adult Services," *ALA Bulletin*, 57:262–66 (March 1963).

Pierce, Bradford K. "The Probable Intellectual and Moral Outcome of the Rapid Increase of Public Libraries," *Library Journal*, 10:234–36 (Sept. 1885).

Powell, John Walker. "One Step Nearer Leadership: Guided Group Reading as a Library Service," *Library Journal*, 71:443–49 (April 1, 1946).

"A Public Library," *Massachusetts Teacher*, 4, no.8:255–56 (Aug. 1851).

"Public Library and the School Are Parts of the Educational System," *Pennsylvania Library Notes*, 2:1–2 (July 1909).

Putnam, Herbert. "Library Development in the Past 20 Years," *Public Libraries*, 16:203–4 (May 1911).

———— "Per Contra," *Library Journal*, 40:471–76 (July 1915).

———— "The Relation of Free Public Libraries to the Community," *North American Review*, 499:663–68 (June 1898).

Rathbone, Josephine A. "The Modern Library Movement," *Public Libraries*, 13: 197–201 (June 1908).

Roden, Carl B. "Ten Years," *Library Journal*, 53:519–25 (June 15, 1928).

Rothrock, Mary U. "Libraries in a New Era," *ALA Bulletin*, 40:227–29 (July 1946).

Rutzen, Ruth. "Detroit's Adult Education Service," *ALA Bulletin*, 31:147–51 (March 1937).

Shera, Jesse H. "On the Value of Library History," *Library Quarterly*, 22: 240–51 (July 1952).

Shirley, Wayne. "What Happened to Our Adult Education Hopes," *Library Journal*, 72:1503–7 (Nov. 1, 1947).

Spofford, Ainsworth. "The Public Libraries of the United States," *Journal of Social Science*, 2:92–114 (1879).

Steiner, Lewis H. "Future of the Free Public Library," *Library Journal*, 15: C44–47 (Dec. 1890).

Stevens, Edward F. "Adult Erudition," *Libraries* (a former publication of Library Bureau, Remington Office Systems, Division of Sperry Rand Corp.), 34:250–54 (June 1929).

Stevenson, Grace. "Libraries Can Help Clubs with Planning Programs," *Library News Bulletin of the Washington State Library*, 16:450–52 (July 1946).

Tyler, Moses Coit. "The Historic Evolution of the Free Public Library in America, and Its True Function in the Community," *Library Journal*, 9:40–47 (March 1884).

Ulveling, Ralph A. "Moving Forward as the People's University," *Public Libraries*, 4:13–16 (March 1950).

Waples, Douglas. "The Relation of Subject Interests to Actual Reading," *Library Quarterly,* 2:42–70 (Jan. 1932).

Wilson, Louis Round. "Library as an Educator," *Library Journal,* 35:6–10 (Jan. 1910).

———— "The Next Fifty Years," *Library Journal,* 61:255–60 (April 1, 1936).

———— "Restudying the Library Chart," *ALA Bulletin,* 30:480–90 (June 1936).

Winsor, Justin. "Free Libraries and Readers," *Library Journal,* 1:63–67 (Sept. 1876).

———— "M. Vattemare and the Public Library System," *Literary World,* 10:185–86 (June 7, 1879).

Reports and Proceedings

American Library Association. *American Heritage Project Annual Report, 1954–55.* Chicago: The Association, 1956.

———— *Experiments in Educational Service for Adults.* Chicago: The Association, 1940. (mimeographed)

———— Office for Adult Education. *Experimental Projects in Adult Education: A Report of the ALA Adult Education Subgrant Project.* Chicago: The Association, 1956.

Asheim, Lester. *Training Needs of Librarians Doing Adult Education Work: A Report of the Allerton Park Conference, November 14–16, 1954.* Chicago: American Library Association, 1955.

Chancellor, John. "The Next Years in Adult Education: Eleventh Annual Report of the Board on the Library and Adult Education, for Ten Months Ending January 31, 1936," *ALA Bulletin,* 30:331–35 (May 1936).

Hewitt, Charles H. *Grant Evaluation Study.* Chicago: American Library Association, 1958. (multilithed)

Report of the Trustees of the Public Library of the City of Boston. City Document No.37, July 1852.

———— City Document No.89, 1875.

Smith, Helen Lyman. *Adult Education Activities in Public Libraries: A Report of the ALA Survey of Adult Education Activities in Public Libraries and State Library Extension Agencies of the United States.* Chicago: American Library Association, 1954.

Warncke, Ruth. "Public Libraries," *Rural Social Systems and Adult Education;* a Committee Report by Charles P. Loomis *et al.* Lansing, Mich.: Michigan State College Pr., 1953.

Wisconsin Free Library Commission. *Proceedings of the Sixth Institute on Public Library Management: Informal Education through Libraries.* Madison: The Commission, 1955. (mimeographed)

Index

A

Access to Public Libraries, 95–96
Adams, Charles Francis, Jr., 16, 26
Adams, John Quincy, 4
Adult Education Activities in Public Libraries, see Smith, Helen Lyman
Adult Education and the Library, 48–49
Adult Education Board, *see* American Library Association. Adult Education Board
Adult Education Roundtable, *see* American Library Association. Adult Education Roundtable
Adult services, 46, 82, 104; literature of, 102–4
Adult Services Division, *see* American Library Association. Adult Services Division
Advisory service, *see* Readers' advisory service
Aged, service to, 98–100, 106–8
Allerton Park Conference, 78, 88
American Heritage Project, *see* American Library Association. American Heritage Project
American Library Association, 14–16, 45–56
  Adult Education Board, 45, 55–56, 68–69, 84–85
  Adult Education Roundtable, 68
  Adult Services Division, 98–100
  American Heritage Project, 73, 86, 88
  Board on the Library and Adult Education, 45, 54–55
  Commission on the Library and Adult Education, 45, 47–54, 67–68; *Libraries and Adult Education,* 51–53, 62
  Enlarged Program, 46
  Library-Community Project, 81–82, 100–102; *Studying the Community,* 101–2
  "National Plan for Libraries, A," 64, 66, 67, 69
  Public Library Service, 74, 79, 89–90
  Small Libraries Project, 96–97
  Subgrant Project, 84
  Wartime activities, 72; postwar activities, 73
Americanization programs, 41
Atomic Energy Institute, Enoch Pratt Free Library, 84

B

Bates, Joshua, 9
Belden, Charles F. D., 53
Berelson, Bernard, 77–78

155

Billings, John Shaw, 37
Birge, Edward A., 33, 37
Bishop, William W., 42, 44
Board on the Library and Adult Education, *see* American Library Association. Board on the Library and Adult Education
Book displays, 41
Book lists, 41, 61, 83, 108
Book promotion, 31
Book talks, 41, 83, 84
Boston Public Library, founding, 4–10
Bostwick, Arthur E., 68
Brett, William Howard, 15, 23, 30
Brown, Walter L., 40, 41
Bryan, James E., 93
Bryson, Lyman L., 59, 62, 66
Buchanan, Scott, 85
Byrnes, Hazel Webster, 58

C

Carnegie, Andrew, 34–36
Carnegie Corporation, 35–36, 43, 46, 47
Cartwright, Morse A., 49
Chamberlain, Arthur H., 37, 40
Chancellor, John, 49, 51, 55, 69, 71
Children's service, 33
Civilian Conservation Corps, 61
Commission on the Library and Adult Education, *see* American Library Association. Commission on the Library and Adult Education
Community-centered libraries, 29
Community services, 61, 80, 83–86
Conference within a Conference, 93–94
Council on Library Resources, Inc., 97
County libraries, 32–33
Craver, Harrison W., 60
"Crime and the Citizen," series of programs, 84
Crunden, Frederick M., 15, 22, 40
Cutter, Charles Ammi, 15, 23, 30, 38; *Rules for a Printed Dictionary Catalogue,* 28

D

Dana, John Cotton, 15, 68
De Vleeschauwer, H. J., *see* Vleeschauwer, H. J., de

Dewey, Melvil, 13, 16, 18–20, 21, 30, 53–54, 63; *The Decimal Classification and Relative Index,* 29
Dimock, Marshall, 66–67
Discussion groups, 49, 55–56, 61–63, 68, 85, 109–110
Displays, 83
Drury, Francis K. W., 55
Dudgeon, Matthew S., 67–68

E

Educational goals, 9–10, 21, 40–42, 56, 82, 104, 114
Educational methods, 67–70
Educational objective, 10, 16–17, 40, 63–65, 76–79, 104, 112–13; barriers to implementation, 17–20, 119–20
Educational role, 10, 20–21, 40, 65–67, 80–82, 104, 113–14
Educational services, 10, 21–24, 40–43, 56–57, 82–88, 104–11, 114–16; suggestions for improving, 120–26
Educational theory and practice, conflict between, 42–43
1852 Report, 7–9
Enlarged Program, *see* American Library Association. Enlarged Program
Everett, Edward, 5–6, 7, 10
Exhibits, 83

F

Farquhar, Alice M., 69
Felsenthal, Emma, *Readable Books in Many Subjects,* 49, 55
Fiction, 12, 24–27, 36–39
Fletcher, William I., 21, 25, 30
Flexner, Jennie M., 49, 71
Foster, William E., 17, 20, 21, 25

G

Gaillard, Edwin W., 41
Goldhor, Herbert, 76
Gray, William S., 49; and Leary, Bernice E., *What Makes a Book Readable,* 59; and Munroe, Ruth, *Reading Interests and Habits of Adults,* 58
Great books, 85, 109–10

Great Decisions program, 109
Great Issues program, 73, 86
Green, Samuel Swett, 15, 17, 22, 24
Gregory, Ruth W., 103, 105, 111
Group services and programs, 61, 83–86, 109, 114–16

H

Hendrick, Burton J., biographer of Andrew Carnegie, 34–35
Henry, Nelson B., ed., *Adult Reading,* 102
Henry, William E., 53
Hill, Frank P., 26
Houle, Cyril O., 75–76, 77, 102
Hubbard, James M., 17

J

Jennings, Judson T., 48, 49, 68, 71
Joeckel, Carleton B., 63, 74
Johnson, Alvin, 67; *The Public Library—A People's University,* 62–63

K

Keppel, Frederick P., 47, 49, 50

L

Lacy, Dan M., 102
Larned, Josephus N., 17, 20
Learned, William S., 47, 48; *The American Public Library and the Diffusion of Knowledge,* 45, 47
Lectures, 41, 56, 110
Leete, John H., 41–42
Leigh, Robert D., 76, 78; *The Public Library in the United States,* 74, 76–79
Lemke, Antje B., ed., *Librarianship and Adult Education,* 103
Libraries and Adult Education, see American Library Association. Commission on the Library and Adult Education
Library adult education, definition of, 78
Library-Community Project, *see* American Library Association. Library-Community Project
Library expansion, 34–36
Library extension, 32–33, 34

Library policies: circulation, hours of opening, open shelves, Sunday opening, 29
Library Services Act, 89–91
Library Services and Construction Act, 91–92
Library 21, 97
Library/USA, 97–98
Library War Service Program (1917–19), 43–46
Lindeman, Eduard C., 53
Locke, George H., 54
Lowell, James Russell, 12, 17, 19
Lyman, Helen H., 103; *see also* Smith, Helen Lyman
Lyndenberg, Harry M., 66

M

McHale, Cecil, 65
McNeal, Archie L., 94
Martin, Everett Dean, 49
Martin, Lowell, 78–79, 83; *Students and the Pratt Library: Challenge and Opportunity,* 93–94
Meyer, Herman H. B., 53
Miller, Robert A., 66
Monroe, Margaret E., *Library Adult Education,* 103
Munn, Ralph, 78
Munroe, Ruth, and Gray, William S., *Reading Interests and Habits of Adults,* 58

N

National Defense Education Act, 93
National Library Week, 97
Novels, *see* Fiction

O

Operational policies, 29
O'Reilly, R. N., 80, 83

P

Peterborough (New Hampshire) Library, 3
Phinney, Eleanor, 98, 104, 105–6, 107; *Library Adult Education in Action,* 102
Pierce, Bradford K., 22
Pioneers in library development, 30
Poole, William Frederick, 15, 25, 30

*Post-War Standards for Public Librar-
ies,* 74–76, 79
Powell, John Walker, 102
Program planning, 41, 84, 86
Public library
    early development, 3
    educational commitment, 1
    need for, 1
    objectives, 74–79
*Public Library in the United States,
The, see* Leigh, Robert D.
Public Library Inquiry, 76, 88
Public Library Service, see American
    Library Association. *Public Li-
    brary Service*
Public schools: criticism of, 19–20;
    purpose, 20
Putnam, Herbert, 28, 38, 41

Q

Quincy, Josiah P., 4, 5, 16, 17, 20

R

Readability Laboratory, Columbia
    University, 59
Reader guidance, *see* Readers' advi-
    sory service
Readers, assistance to, 21
Readers' advisory service, 46, 57–61,
    83, 109
"Reading for an Age of Change" se-
    ries, 99
Reading improvement programs, 110–
    11
"Reading with a Purpose" series, 49–
    51
Recordings, 108
Recreational objective, 24–27, 36–39,
    42–43, 78
Recreational reading, *see* Recreational
    objective
Reference objective, 27–28, 42–43
Reference service, 39, 43
Richardson, Ernest C., 40
Robinson, Edward S., 68–69
Roden, Carl, 54
Rose, Ernestine, 68

S

Seaver, Benjamin, 9
Segregation in public libraries, 94–96
Shera, Jesse H., 7

Sherman, Clarence E., 60–61, 64–65
Small Libraries Project, *see* American
    Library Association. Small Li-
    braries Project
Smith, Helen Lyman, *Adult Educa-
    tion Activities in Public Librar-
    ies,* 88
Steiner, Lewis H., 23
Stevens, Edward F., 50
Stevenson, Grace T., 103, 104
Stone, C. Walter, 103, 104
Student service, 92–94
Subgrant Project, *see* American Li-
    brary Association. Subgrant Proj-
    ect

T

Technical processes, 28–29
Thorndike, Edward L., 49
Ticknor, George, 6, 7, 10
Titcomb, Mary L., 32
Tompkins, Miriam, 71
Traveling libraries, 32
Tyler, Moses C., 17
Tyler, Ralph W., and Waples, Doug-
    las, *What People Want To Read
    About,* 58

U

U.S. Bureau of Education, special re-
    port on libraries, 19
Utley, Henry Munson, 15, 17, 18, 30,
    33

V

Vattemare, M. Nicholas Marie Alex-
    andre, 4
Victory Book Campaign, 73
Vitz, Carl, 73
Vleeschauwer, H. J., de, 39

W

Waples, Douglas, and Tyler, Ralph W.,
    *What People Want To Read
    About,* 58
Wessells, Helen E., *The Public Li-
    brary for Lifelong Learning,* 103
Wheeler, Joseph L., 76, 97
Wight, John B., Reverend, 5
Wilson, Louis R., 66
Winsor, Justin, 15, 29, 30